D0070316

Mary Mellish
Archibald
Memorial

THE OPEN NIGHT

By the same Author

THE AGE OF THE DRAGON
Poems, 1930–1951

THE OPEN NIGHT

John Lehmann

Here is the place my Lord, good my Lord enter,
The tirrany of the open night's too rough
For Nature to endure. [Storme still]
King Lear

LONGMANS, GREEN AND CO
LONDON . NEW YORK . TORONTO

1952

Mary Mellish
Archibald
Memorial

LONGMANS GREEN AND CO LTD
6 & 7 CLIFFORD STREET LONDON W 1

ALSO AT MELBOURNE AND CAPE TOWN

LONGMANS GREEN AND CO INC
55 FIFTH AVENUE NEW YORK 3

LONGMANS GREEN AND CO
215 VICTORIA STREET TORONTO 1

ORIENT LONGMANS LTD
BOMBAY CALCUTTA MADRAS

First published 1952

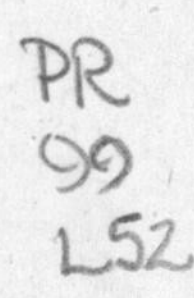

Printed in Great Britain by
Latimer, Trend & Co. Ltd., Plymouth

Foreword

I have collected in this book a handful of essays, all of which deal with writers who died during my lifetime, and whose work, at one time or another, I devoured as the only dish my hunger demanded. Some of these writers were younger at the time of their death than a number of writers of equal or greater significance who are still alive, and to whom I have also, in print or on the air, at one time or another during the last ten years, offered my homage; but I have kept here to those whose work can be viewed in its completeness and about whom one can speak without evasion or concealment.

Several of the writers I have chosen were poets in the strict sense of the word, that is, they wrote in verse; but the others seem to me to have been, in a wider interpretation, also poets, endeavouring in prose to solve what are essentially a poet's problems. And it is through a certain conception of poetry that I believe these essays to be linked into a coherent whole, as the exposition of an attitude towards literature and life, shaped by the nature of the world we live in and the late hour to which the hands of history point. Two themes are intertwined in them: the attempt to evaluate the meaning of poetry in our lives, and the examination of the way poets themselves have thought their lives should be ordered in order to serve poetry. Thus it is that, within these limits, this book has also become the story of a search for the motives and ideals that underlie the life-pattern of men and women of genius who have lived through the stresses of our age.

I have added to the essays two lectures, which I gave both in Europe and South America during the last few years under the auspices of The British Council, and which deal in a more general and explicit way with these preoccupations. If they had been essays

A 590 14

I would perhaps have rewritten them entirely, in order at least to bring them up-to-date; as it is, I have, with some small alterations dictated by reflection at the time, and some small excisions to prevent overlapping, left them as they were spoken.

Many of these essays appeared originally in *New Writing*, and for those, therefore, which were printed in the Penguin series, my acknowledgements are due to Penguin Books. Acknowledgements are also due to *World Review*, and to the B.B.C., for whom, in their commissioned form as broadcast scripts, *But for Beaumont Hamel* and *A Human Standpoint* were originally prepared.

JOHN LEHMANN

Acknowledgments

My acknowledgments and thanks are due to the following: Dr. Edith Sitwell and Messrs. Macmillan and Co. Ltd., for permission to quote material from *The Canticle of the Rose*; Mrs. W. B. Yeats, Messrs. Macmillan and Co. Ltd., and the Macmillan Company of Canada for material from *The Collected Poems of W. B. Yeats*; Messrs. Faber and Faber Ltd. for extracts from the works of T. S. Eliot; Messrs. Chatto and Windus and Messrs. A. M. Heath and Co. Ltd., for quotations from C. K. Scott-Moncrieff's translation of Proust; Messrs. George Allen and Unwin Ltd., for material from the works of the late Alun Lewis; Miss Mary Owen and Messrs. Chatto and Windus for quotations from the works of the late Wilfred Owen; Mrs. Edward Thomas for material from the poems and prose of the late Edward Thomas; Messrs. Sidgwick and Jackson Ltd. for extracts from the works of Rupert Brooke; Messrs. J. M. Dent and Sons Ltd. for quotations from Joseph Conrad's *The Rover*; Mr. Innes Rose and Messrs. John Farquharson Ltd. for material from the work of Henry James; and Mr. Leonard Woolf and The Hogarth Press for material from the work of Virginia Woolf.

for
ROSAMOND

Contents

Mary Mellish
Archibald
Memorial

The Search for the Myth*

Not very long ago I was re-reading that fantastic and wonderful book *The Golden Ass* by Lucius Apuleius, and I was struck, quite unexpectedly, by something extraordinarily modern about it. To-day, of course, we find Apuleius's unquestioning acceptance of witches and the evil spells they can cast on men, and the grotesque things you have to do to escape from their clutches, we find all that very strange, very much of his time and not of ours: but I am thinking of his interest in symbolism and myth-making. *The Marriage of Cupid and Psyche* is one of the most beautiful stories that have come down to us from the Ancient World, and it is also one of the subtlest and most poetic of allegories; and the great climax of the book with its invocation to Isis and the celebration of her rites, in spite of much that has lost its significance for us in our Christian world, is written with such fervour and brilliance that we feel behind the symbols the apprehension of mysterious and eternal truths.

All living creatures that are capable of it crave symbols; even a dog is indulging in a kind of symbolism if it takes its master's slipper to its basket to console it when its master has gone away; even the crudest early religious practices are attempts on the part of primitive men to give a concrete shape and permanence to ideas, glimpses of truth and beauty that have come to them in their moments of deepest reflection or illumination, which they feel they may lose sight of unless they are seized and imprisoned—like living creatures under Midas's golden touch—in image and dramatic pattern. We know little enough of the Eleusinian Mysteries and yet the little we know, the tantalizing hints we find among the tragic, violated ruins at Eleusis makes us feel that they, with

* A Lecture delivered at Athens, November 1946.

the Orphic Mysteries, were the supreme expression of myth-making power in the Ancient World. The dog recreates the master who has vanished from the slipper he has left behind; and, at the other end of the scale, poetry—in Shelley's words—'redeems from decay the visitations of the divinity in man'. The poet transfigures what he experiences with his senses, what he sees, hears and touches, into symbols of some reality behind the senses, a reality of the spirit. Baudelaire gave us the classic expression of this, when he wrote:

> La Nature est un temple où de vivants piliers
> Laissent parfois sortir de confuses paroles
> L'homme y passe à travers des forêts de symboles
> Qui l'observent avec des regards familiers. . . .

We cannot do without symbols. Nor can we escape them. The industrial towns and cities in which most of us pass our lives are so full of ugly symbols, which say such false things about the nature of existence, that we long to destroy them, or break away from them. Sometimes this desire is altogether incoherent and unacknowledged. Perhaps the droning, death-laden bomber which haunted the world in days and nights that are still all too vivid for most of us, is even the obscure creation of a hatred of modern symbols that imprison us, an impulse of destruction buried well below the surface of the minds of highly civilized people to-day. Again, I have heard many young men say that the war, terrible though it was in its essence, was welcome to them because it transported them from the confinement of false and hateful symbols to surroundings that more truly expressed what they felt to be the nature of man's life in the world: to the small ship in the limitless, dangerous sea, to the camp in the desert, to the tangled track through the inexhaustible jungle.

If *The Golden Ass* seemed to me peculiarly modern, then, it was because the search for new symbols and myths is so intense a preoccupation in the literature and art of our times, and so important in what is valued in the heritage of the past by the young poets and intellectuals, not merely in one country today but I believe in the whole of Europe—and America, too, if we are to judge from what is characteristic of the latest school of young writers, the successors of Hemingway and Dos Passos. It is evident in the popularity of authors such as Kafka and Rilke and Herman Melville, in Paris and Geneva and Rome as well as London; in the innumerable critical studies and interpretations of these authors which appear in the avant-garde reviews in so many different languages. It can be traced by the decline of interest in naturalism and that straightforward realism which had so widespread (and perhaps necessary) a vogue in the thirties.

The reason for this return to the kind of art that conceals a metaphysical meaning behind and above what it states, is surely not far to seek. As in the outside world, so in the realm of the mind. For many hundreds of thousands of Europeans, of course, the Christian religion is still a completely adequate source of symbols, and the craving of their imagination is satisfied by the story of Christ, the parables of the New Testament, and the religious art they find in their churches; but traditional Christianity's hold on the mind of Europe has nevertheless been weakening over many decades, and two world wars have immensely accelerated the process. Between the wars, one might have said as a fairly accurate generalization that a materialistic view of life had gained the upper hand, beneath a superficial façade of Christian conformity; and in some parts of the world the façade had been discarded altogether, and materialism had become a dogma—even a persecuting dogma.

Today, I believe, that is changing. Mankind is confronted by vaster dangers, more bewildering problems than ever before. The assumptions behind the confident machine-civilization of the West are being questioned in the light of the obvious, the appalling failure of that civilization to fulfil its promises and justify the untold human sacrifice and effort that has gone to its making in a century and a half of industrial expansion and competition. The collective materialism that has challenged the West does not any longer seem so certain a way out of the impasse: to the philosopher and poet indeed it is beginning to appear a kind of despair. Abandoning the metaphysic of religion while retaining the fanaticism of the ancient creeds, it has denied the mystery, it has not solved it. But life, we feel now, among our ruined cities, is more complex and more mysterious than the textbooks of progress ever told us, and we look round for symbols that shall recreate faith within the enlarged circumference of this new awareness.

Such a moment is Christianity's opportunity. And it is true that the Catholic Church in the West has gained new strength since the onslaught of Nazi nihilism was defeated: startling new strength if we are to accept without closer examination the success of parties with Catholic backing at the elections in many countries. And yet, for wide masses of people the Christian symbols as they have known them have ceased to be significant, and their desperate need is to find new symbols—even if those symbols should lead us back to a rediscovery of the central meaning of Christianity, restored through the discarding of outworn and corrupted images, and irrelevant secretions of idea.

In the collapse of traditional religion, in the silence of the creative religious impulse, it is on the poet that the responsibility falls to make a world of true symbols, and to find a new myth for mankind to inhabit. And by the poet, I mean not merely the artist who uses verse as his medium of expression, but also the artist who uses prose for the same ends—the ends of the creative imagination—whose prose, in fact, means more than it says.

I think it is true to say that the greatest poets have always striven to create a myth, a world that shall be a symbol for the world of actual existence in its moral and aesthetic aspects. Some poets have only succeeded in making a myth for their age, the smallest poets for the fashion of a few years; but the poets who shine most brilliantly in the firmament of our European literature have created myths or transformed the legends and religious symbols of their time into myths of their own, that still have power over us today. Such are Homer, Virgil, Dante; Shakespeare with his soaring power created not only one but many myths, for Hamlet and Macbeth and Prospero's Island are separately part of European consciousness, though it is possible to say that the whole of Shakespearean tragedy is one vast myth in many facets; Milton toyed with the idea of using the King Arthur legends for his epic, but chose in the end—as I believe to our great good fortune—the framework of the Biblical myth of creation to create his own sublime myth of the battle of good and evil; Shelley perhaps more completely than any other great poet, invented his own myth with his own symbols, and that is why *Prometheus Unbound* has such obscurity and complexity in its beauty; Rimbaud, like Byron before him, completed his myth by living it, so that power comes from both together and one cannot think of the poetry without the life or the life without the colouring of the poetry; and the whole seems to have passed into the eternity of symbols from the wastage of time.

I do not believe it is necessary for the poet to be entirely conscious of this responsibility that lies upon him in our age, to create the symbols by which man can save himself from despair. The poet is a medium through which the needs of an age make themselves felt before they are formulated, and he may be aware of them only as a creative urgency in his imagination, as the green tip of a bulb pushes up through the earth with its hidden colour and shape of flowering to come; but a formulated awareness may nevertheless help to stimulate what is already growing, may encourage tending and dedication. It may, of course, at the same time encourage bad poets to create pretentious and feeble myths, but that is an unimportant price to pay if the true poet has also seen his work lying more clearly ahead of him. A critic should not be afraid to call out like John the Baptist, even though there have been many Baptists whose call has never been answered; if the poet he is looking for is there he can only have given him aid, not harmed him.

And if we look round at the landscape of modern literature, what signs do we see that there are poets who are working to fulfil this need in our time? I do not merely mean living poets, for sometimes a poet's work only reveals its full significance after the breathing poet is dead; and then the gradual revealing of the beauty and value of what he wrote is as if he were still writing, still alive with unknown discoveries still to be made for the world—as if the 'living hand' of Keats's famous unfinished lines, were still 'warm and capable' and moving across the paper in its creative work. It is not that such a poet's work has been neglected in his own lifetime; such an explanation is too simple, and misses the point, that the conditions in relation to which the poet was writing did not exist during his lifetime: but only come into existence gradually, at a later date. What stranger or more terrible story is there than that of the broken, dying Rimbaud passing unknown through France on his way home, while the advanced literary circles of the capital were beginning to discover his genius, to give him that fame he had craved so many years before; but the poet was dead, long buried in the sands of Africa, even though the tortured body was lingering on. Sometimes when one is travelling in an aeroplane above the cloud ceiling, the shadow of the aeroplane is cast on the insubstantial mother-of-pearl sea-billows far ahead, distinct with a ghostly motion of its own, while directly below the aeroplane itself there is no shadow at all. So the shadow of the poet's message is cast sometimes on the dimension of time far ahead of his own life. Such poets and poet-philosophers can be found in every literature; it is probably true that Dostoievski—at least for England and America where Constance Garnett's translations only began to appear a little more than a generation ago—has enormously more significance today than during his lifetime, for *The Brothers Karamazov*, with its subtle use of dreams and stories that lift the narrative to the plane of poetry, seems to us more myth than reality, nearer to a Greek tragedy than to the type of the nineteenth-century novel; a more unquestionable example is Soren Kierkegaard, surely as much poet as philosopher, for what is more startling than the ferment his thought has produced in our intellectual world today, so long after his death? In our own Anglo-Saxon literature we can point to John Keats, hardly known except to a handful of friends during his life and scorned by the reigning schools of taste; perhaps Herman Melville, too, for there is little to suggest that his own times found in his work what we today find, to whom the White Whale Moby Dick and his battles with Captain Ahab have become one of the great myths, and *Billy Budd* an essay in symbolism for which there is no parallel in daring and complexity among Melville's contemporaries.

One can think of several short novels written during the last half century or so which have something of the same quality, a concentrated symbolic quality: Thomas Mann's *Death in Venice* for instance, and Ivan Bunin's *The Gentleman from San Francisco* and Henry James's *The Turn of the Screw*, but none of them has the force and passion of Melville's *Billy Budd*, none probes more dangerously below the surface of our human destiny.

Herman Melville indeed is a living poet in the truest sense of the word for my contemporaries in England today; and, as I have already mentioned, those two great writers of the dying Habsburg Empire, Rainer Maria Rilke and Franz Kafka, are alive for us in the same way; rather because it is only recently that their works have begun to be translated into English, so that these translations —like the Garnett translations from Dostoievski before the First World War—come to us with the force of a contemporary poet's work, than because they were not fully appreciated in their own language when they wrote. Both writers have deeply influenced the younger generation of our poets and novelists—perhaps only publishers and editors, who see the innumerable manuscripts that never get into print, can gauge how deeply.

Rilke's influence is all-pervasive in our modern poetry: his power of recreating ancient legends, such as that of the Prodigal Son or Orpheus and Eurydice, of taking some of the oldest symbols, such as that of the Angel, and infusing them with a new personal significance and beauty, have been—continue indeed to be —an inspiration both direct and indirect to almost all the outstanding poets in our country; something of Rilke's spirit has passed, I believe, into the work of Edith Sitwell, of Stephen Spender, of Cecil Day Lewis, of Louis MacNeice, of Terence Tiller—and many others one could name.

As for Kafka, at least two young English writers of note, Rex Warner and William Sansom show the mark of his strange myth-creating art; William Sansom, I think, more obviously. Some of his stories reveal an extraordinary power of creating a nightmare world of symbols out of the ordinary world. I remember when I was a very small boy I had a dream which I can still recall vividly; our whole family, my parents, my sisters and myself were in the dining-room at home eating breakfast, when a huge white-headed crow or raven walked in through the window from the garden, and we were all overcome with a feeling of intense excitement, a certainty that this represented something of awe-inspiring significance. I can find no explanation for the dream:* and I can find no explanation—no tidy explanation that is—for some of Sansom's imagined happenings, which have just the same effect on my adult mind. In other stories Sansom tries to explain his purpose too clearly, and loses enormously in power: a poem, a myth should be *felt* to be true and beautiful rather than rationally understood; Psyche's lover vanishes from her embrace when she takes the light to scrutinize him too closely.

* My sister Rosamond tells me now that there was an actual white-headed crow in our garden for years.

How unfathomable the promptings of the creative imagination are, and how mysteriously ideas succeed in floating, like invisible thistledown, across frontiers; while Sansom was writing in London, a young French writer in his own poetic laboratory across the Channel, Noël Devaulx, had been experimenting with the same kind of symbols, producing stories of an eerie allegorical power; and yet he can hardly have known about Sansom's writing, as both were making their reputations when the war divided England and France into separate, almost sound-proof, compartments.

I think I should add at this point that there are, as I see it, two kinds of myth-making in literature. There is the kind I have been talking about hitherto, in which the characters and scenes—if it is a story—are symbols of something beyond them; such as Cupid and Psyche in Apuleuis's tale, and Billy Budd and Captain Vere in Melville's novel. There is another kind in which an author takes a certain type of man or kind of life—it may be in his own day, it may be in the past, or even only in legend—and by engaging our sympathies intensely in his creation produces an ideal magnetic image that may profoundly affect the way men judge and act. How many images of this nature, responding to the inchoate longings of the age, were created in the years that followed the Napoleonic Wars. In our own day, such eminent writers as Ernest Hemingway, in *For Whom the Bell Tolls*, and André Malraux, in *Espoir* and *Le Temps du Mépris*, have attempted a similar task, exalting the man of revolutionary violence who is also an intellectual as the Aeneas of the twentieth century.

When the liberation of France at last restored intellectual contact between our two countries, we found that, while writers of established and European reputation—André Gide, François Mauriac and André Malraux—were still active and still held in high esteem, a new group of writers had come into spotlight prominence of a very different outlook, who were engaged in just this second kind of myth-making.

If we take the two most prominent, Jean-Paul Sartre and Albert Camus, we see that both—however much they differ in their interpretation of the fashionable existentialist philosophy—are endeavouring to exalt certain types of men, certain kinds of conduct to express their view of the world, and have turned to old legends and periods of history imprecise enough to be remoulded according to their own ideas, to serve as their vehicles. Sartre is, of course, a writer of brilliant power, and Camus, a much younger man, has still the promise of an exciting future;* and yet, to the English expectation at any rate, there is something curiously unsatisfying about the world they present, the moral they wish to point. There is a denial of human responsibility, a contempt for human respect which might be astringent in a Europe suffering from a sentimental excess of brotherly love. But when, in the memories of the oldest amongst us, has Europe been in such a state? Certainly not to-day. Nor is the mood of Sartre, Camus and their followers the mood of other great French writers of our time, such as Malraux, or Mauriac, or Gide, or Supervielle, or Saint-Exupéry who was killed during the war.

Ten years ago, it is interesting to remember, D. H. Lawrence, novelist and poet, was still one of the great names in modern English literature. Towards the end of his life he almost completely abandoned the realistic novel in his search for a new creed, a new myth. He travelled all over the world in the endeavour to find something outside and before Christianity that would supply him with symbols to put in the place of what he felt was weak and hateful in the Christian creed. The preacher got the upper hand of the artist for a long time; yet in the end the artist succeeded in creating works of extraordinary symbolic power, such as *The Woman Who Rode Away* and *The Man Who Died*. In spite of this, Lawrence means surprisingly little today to the younger generation in England. A Lawrence enthusiast would say, perhaps, that it is simply because his books have been all but unobtainable for so long and a revival will come when they are printed again.† Lawrence is indeed, at his best, an amazing artist, and for that he will again be given due honour in the course of time; but I cannot help feeling that his present eclipse may have other reasons. We have fought the Satanism of Hitler for seven years; we have come to recognize that the precious ore in the values that our own

* *The Plague* had not been published at the time this lecture was written: it seems to me infinitely to surpass *The Outsider*, and would force me to modify my judgement on Camus's work if I were to rewrite this lecture today.

† Since I wrote this, Penguin Books have, of course, made their dramatic bid to bring the best of his work within the reach of thousands who have never read him before.

Christian heritage has brought with it is more important than the dross. Can the myth which we are looking for be a denial of the world of love? Should it not rather be an exploration of that world? It is not new creeds, the worship of a barbaric plumed serpent, that we crave: but the restatement of some of the most ancient truths of our civilization within the conditions of our modern life.

A poet of course may create a myth in every poem he writes; certainly even a short poem can have the force of a long story, such as *Death in Venice*, if a great poet writes it. In this century I expect you will all be able to think of poems by Rilke, Lorca, Valéry, Apollinaire and Yeats that have this particular kind of concentrated force. There are songs in Shakespeare's plays that seem like a distillation of an immeasurable wealth of experience. A single poem may sometimes live into posterity out of a poet's work, and its myth become part of the spiritual life of generation after generation. Such cases, however, are rare; and the problem which faces the poet who wishes to establish his symbols with an enduring life in the imagination of men, is either to create a drama of symbols (and that is a myth), or a system of symbols which every new poem he writes explores further and helps to complete. Such a sequence of myth-making poems Rilke has given us in his *Duino Elegies*, which is rightly looked upon as the supreme expression of his genius. In *The Waste Land*, T. S. Eliot, using a basic pattern of the Grail Legend and its remoter prototypes of the ancient world, showed what a master he was in the use of symbols underlying a large and complex poetic work; in his latest work, *Four Quartets*, which was published section by section during the war—each section as exciting to many of us as news of a great victory—an elaborate system of personal and Christian symbols is woven in and out of the poems in an intricate dance of deeply satisfying beauty.

Four Quartets is a work of amazing sheer poetic radiation and intellectual vigour; and yet it has the disadvantage that one cannot live in it as one lives in *The Tempest* or *Paradise Lost*: the effect, one might say, is more like that of a magnificent Persian carpet than a painted picture. The system of symbols which Edith Sitwell, on the other hand, has explored with such wonderful results in her poetry of the last seven years, is as consistent as Eliot's, and though it may lack the strong-girdered intellectual structure of his work, it does, I think, succeed in evoking an inhabitable literary world. If one opens the book *A Song of the Cold* at the very first page, one is introduced to this world with the swift shock of surprise and wonder that one has when the curtain goes up on the first scene of a great new ballet in a darkened theatre:

> I who was once a golden woman like those who walk
> In the dark heavens—but am now grown old
> And sit by the fire and see the fire grow cold,
> Watch the dark fields for a rebirth of faith and wonder.
>
> The turning of Ixion's wheel the day
> Ceased not, yet sounds no more the beat of the heart
> But only the sound of the ultimate darkness falling
> And of the Blind Samson at the Fair, shaking the pillars of the
> world and emptily calling.
>
> For the gardener cried for rain, but the high priests howled
> For a darker rain to cool the delirium of gold
> And wash the sore of the world, the heart of Dives,
> Raise wheat for the hunger that lies in the soul of the poor——
> Then came the thunderous darkness. . . .

I do not think there is any other example in our own poetry today that can be compared, in myth-making power, with T. S. Eliot's *Four Quartets* or Edith Sitwell's *Song of the Cold*. Nevertheless a number of young poets—and I would instance Dylan Thomas, Lawrence Durrell, Terence Tiller and Henry Reed as outstanding among many others—have already shown that they can use symbols to produce effects that are rich in imaginative suggestion, and rich in promise too. I know a little, through translation, of modern Greek poetry, and have been deeply impressed by the presence of just this quality I have been speaking of; indeed what I have read of the work of Sikelianos, Seferis and Elytis, poems such as *The Death Feast of the Greeks*, *Mythistorima*, and *The Age of Blue Memory*, lead me to the conclusion that there is a poetic renaissance in Greece at this time* which few countries of Europe can rival, and which may, as it gradually becomes known in other countries through the work of devoted translators, have

* I am speaking here of the work of living poets, of course, or I would necessarily have dealt with the supremely great work of Constantine Cavafy.

a richly fertilizing effect on the course of modern poetry, on that work of myth-making which I believe to be so high a responsibility of the poet today. And in connection with this, I am reminded that it was the novel use of symbols and the pure economy, the dark and passionate sincerity with which they were used, that first brought startled attention a few years ago to the poems which Demetrios Capetanakis began writing in English—with a command of English that we still find almost inexplicable in a Greek who had been living with us for only so short a time. Such poems as *Abel*, *The Isles of Greece*, *Detective Story*, and *Lazarus* are among the most memorable poetic achievements of the war years in England.

I do not want to suggest that the poet in the strict sense of the word, or the artist in words, is the only creator who can provide us with the spiritual food we need. To me the poet is the most important, because words can suggest impressions of all the senses and can speak to the intellect at the same time as they are speaking to the imagination; but I recognize that to many people the language of music penetrates further and creates a world, complete in itself, of more intense beauty; and to others colour and form are the medium through which they can live in myth and symbol. The visions of reality that Michelangelo and Poussin, to take two outstanding examples, have given us in their paintings are among the most precious possessions of the European spirit; and if I rate them a little below what Aeschylus, Dante and Shakespeare have given us, I hold them nevertheless as amongst the most inspired achievements of the myth-making imagination. In modern art we have the romantic myths of the subconscious created by Salvador Dali out of symbols which in the hands of innumerable Surrealist imitators have become little more than fashionable counters of correct sensibility, just as urns and pilasters were in the eighteenth century; we have Chirico's wild-maned noble horses, which for all their fascination seem too limited a symbol to bear a whole vision of the world; and we have the extraordinary and exquisite symbolism of Paul Klee, too private perhaps ever to capture the European mind. In Britain, Henry Moore and Graham Sutherland among the artists of a new generation, have, each in his own entirely individual way, set out on a quest for a world of symbols to express a powerful imagination looking below the visible surface of life to find what Shelley called 'forms more real than living man'; in

Greece, too, I have seen the works of modern artists, above all the works of Ghika, which are charged with powerful individual symbolism. I am reminded of what Capetanakis said of Ghika's work at the second Pan-Hellenic Art Exhibition:

> Ghika's symbols no longer have the general abstract character, which they had till now. They are closely linked with the soil and sky of a definite place. But it is just for that reason that their artistic significance has increased. The more precise the language of art becomes the wider becomes its meaning and the deeper. . . . The straight line, the broken line, the curve are symbols to him which illuminate our path with a light from another universe. His painting struggles to be a symbol of all that is highest. And in that it differs from surrealism. Surrealism is also a realization of symbols, but their purpose is to express the depths which are found beneath the individual consciousness. The symbols of Ghika's painting try, on the contrary, to express the heights which are beyond all consciousness. Surrealism turns the eye downwards, Ghika's painting turns it upward. . . .

Here, I think, is the heart of the matter. We are not looking simply for symbols of the dark forces that exist—that can exist in the universe. We are rather looking for symbols 'of all that is highest', symbols that are, as I have said, a new exploration of the world of love, the embodiment of the deepest moral law of the universe, that reasserts itself in *Macbeth* to destroy the tyrant and in *King Lear* to pluck triumph and exultation out of tragedy. Lawrence taught us, as a corrective to a culture that has come to rely too much on its rational powers, the great danger of ignoring the instinctual forces; what history has taught us during the last ten years is the danger that may come from these instinctual forces if not controlled by moral law—if not integrated in the world of love—because the instinctual can be both good and evil.

We cannot escape symbols: in the spiritual world we live by them as a blind man finds his way with his stick that taps the pavement. We crave symbols so much that if we are not presented with symbols of beauty and truth by those who can see more clearly into the mysteries of existence, we will take symbols of what is really evil, that lure us—with the promise of escape from hateful and inadequate symbols—to our destruction. That is surely what happened to a whole generation that followed the false symbols of fascism, the evil myth that has laid Europe in ruins. That is why the symbols of beauty and truth are so desperately needed today. It may be that the fundamental myth is always the same. I can understand those who say that in the great literatures and philosophies of the world all aspects of that myth have been explored, and all we need is to acquaint ourselves with them by long and patient study; but I do not agree with them. Each poet writes within the material surroundings of his age, and these surroundings have changed during the last five hundred years at an accelerating pace. Each change presents a field for new symbols; and only new symbols, or a new arrangement of ancient symbols can give us that shock of simultaneous recognition and wonder that fully captures our imagination and opens it to the action of art. Without the heritage of the great poets of the past we should indeed be lost in the wilderness, but without the work of the poets of our own time we might even lose sight of that heritage, unable to distinguish where it stood in the landscape of our lives, our civilization. There lies the poet's great opportunity today, and his great responsibility; and the responsibility of the critic, who can help to create the ferment of ideas which may bring the poet to his fullest expression, and can also train his vision to recognize his coming from far away.

The world today looks in a kind of paralysed dread at the supreme achievement of its own science, the absolute agent of pure destruction, the atom bomb. The spirit which would oppose all that the atom bomb stands for may indeed be appalled at the enormous resources, the vast and complex organization, the multitude of men of high intellectual endowment, demanded by the production of that satanic agency; and may wonder whether it can ever confront it with any equivalent power that will work for Eros. And yet what greater power can that spirit call upon, than the small, so insignificant-seeming word, the creative word, the word of the poet?

The Man Who Learnt to Walk Naked

Like all the poets of my generation, I have worshipped at the shrine of W. B. Yeats. I fell heavily for *The Lake Isle of Innisfree* when I was a small boy at my private school: and I have gone on reading him with devotion ever since, poems, plays, autobiographies and other prose works, but always the poems above all. No wonder, then, that the few occasions on which I was privileged to see him, or hear him speak, have remained in my memory as pictures with a special glow and holiness. The last occasion I remember particularly clearly; it was in a London club, a year or two before the war, and he was sitting in the middle of the huge pillared drawing-room, alone, with a book in his lap. He was not reading the book, because he had fallen asleep; but even in this rather unexpected impromptu nap he looked, to me, very noble and very romantic, as if he must be dreaming of Cuchulain, and the cloths of heaven, and the wild swans at Coole. Oddly enough, however, owing to some previous train of thought I have long since forgotten, his lines to an Irish airman came into my mind at that moment:

> Nor law, nor duty bade me fight,
> Nor public men, nor cheering crowds,
> A lonely impulse of delight
> Drove to this tumult in the clouds. . . .

And it struck me then, as it still strikes me now, that what was so impressive about him was that he too, in his own poet's way, had been true all his life to a 'lonely impulse of delight', and in an age about as inimical to such a faith as anyone can find in history. In his very first volume, in 1889, he had announced, striking something a little more sincere than the fashionable attitudes of the day, in the poem called *The Song of the Happy Shepherd*, that 'words alone are certain good'; and through all the artistic and political movements with which he came to be associated that idea remained his lodestone. He did not cut himself off from the clamour and violence and passionate partisanship that resulted in his country's independence, but he never let those things shout down the voice of poetry inside him. Other poets have taken to prose or public affairs because their ambitions could not be satisfied with the small fame such a lone calling could bring them, or because they were not strong enough, or convinced enough about the ultimate worth of poetry to swim against the stream; but the springs of Yeats's inspiration remained unmuddied through dangers that a great contemporary of his could ward off only through exile; and what is even more significant, they never dried up. A dedication so unwavering—and at the same time so successful—is almost without parallel in our distracted times.

It is, of course, this faith in poetry, and the continuity of his expression of it, that has made Yeats so powerful an influence on the younger poets who began writing during the last twenty years. But to say that is only to state a remarkable fact in its most general terms; and the attraction has been so magically strong, that anyone who wants to understand the meaning and action of poetry in the sum total of life must try to examine it a little more closely.

If one reads through the sequence of Yeats's poetry, from the beginning with *Crossways* to *The King of the Great Clock Tower* and the final poems before his death, one is bound to recognize that his start was so brilliant, that if he had only been known by his first two volumes, if he had died fifty years ago after the publication of *The Rose*, he would still have been outstanding and would still have been quoted and represented in every anthology today; but what made him so dominating a figure is that he went on living and his art went on developing, both in its technical mastery and in its content. He has summed up that development himself, in his own inimitably pithy way:

> I made my songs a coat
> Covered with embroideries
> Out of old mythologies
> From heel to throat;

But the fools caught it,
Wore it in the world's eyes
As though they'd wrought it.
Song, let them take it,
For there's more enterprise
In walking naked.

Like some other great artists, he disconcerted his followers by abandoning his early manner just when they had made themselves proficient copyists of it, and the wonderful embroideries he fished up from the deep chest of Irish legend and ancient myth, and re-fashioned with a craft learnt from the pre-Raphaelites and symbolists, but already entirely his own in the early nineties, he abandoned for that 'walking naked' which is the chief miracle of the phase that followed the 1914 war. It was not enough simply to live on; other poets have lived into middle and old age, and left their art way behind them in the tomb; but by growing as an artist as well, he achieved what so many young Romantics have been denied by death; what Chatterton and Shelley and Keats a hundred years before and the poets of the 1914 war in his own time could only promise. And by his amazingly complete flowering he preserved his early work in all its freshness, for such lyrical masterpieces as *Innisfree* and *Wandering Aengus*, which might by themselves have seemed cloying to a latter-day taste, acquire a new interest, a new life when related to *Meditation in Time of Civil War* and *Coole and Ballylee*, becoming part of a crown of achievement greater than any of its individual jewels. All the cunning he had learnt in his craft as a young man, all the intensity of dream which made the visions of the Irish renaissance pass into the artistic consciousness of the modern world, were reborn into a new wisdom, a maturity of heart and mind enriched by the experience not merely of a cycle of love, but of public affairs, of contact with many men of many kinds that the theatre, and war, and revolution on his doorstep brought him. William Wordsworth is probably the very last poet in the world the sumptuous embroideries of *Crossways* and *The Rose* would call to mind; and yet it is precisely the Wordsworth who wrote the famous Sonnets of 1802 that I am reminded of when I read such a poem by the mature Yeats as *Nineteen Hundred and Nineteen*:

> We too had many pretty toys when young:
> A law indifferent to blame or praise,
> To bribe or threat; habit that made old wrong
> Melt down, as it were wax in the Sun's rays;
> Public opinion ripening for so long
> We thought it would outlive all future days.
> O what fine thought we had because we thought
> That the worst rogues and rascals had died out. . . .

One may believe that Wordsworth, in the final reckoning, is the greater poetic phenomenon; and yet it is apposite to remember that the author of the *Ode on Intimations of Immortality* showed no such continuity of growth and harvest, and that by the time he had reached the age when Yeats wrote *Byzantium* he had become an almost unreadable old bore.

This evolution then, the way in which the young Romantic who began by singing of 'eternal beauty wandering on her way' while Kipling was thumping out his tunes for Tommy Atkins, learnt to transpose his marvellous music into another key, and present us with a symbol-figure of a poet whose ivory tower of dreams became the real tower from which he could hear the cry of 'Vengeance for Jacques Molay'—this maturing into Delphic utterance is one of the chief sources of his power over the minds of contemporary poets. But behind it all, of course, was the supreme craftsmanship, compounded of so many elements which one is apt to overlook as one enjoys the effortless splendour of his lines. Yeats had the great advantage of starting with a special territory of his own, the woods and mountains and wild shores where Fergus and Cuchulain and Niamh celebrated their loves and sorrows and heroic battles, and the singer was forever in quest of 'the red rose-bordered hem'; but he could not have established his claim to this territory so successfully if he had not, as all great poets, invented his own music, his own recognizable voice as a poet, almost from the beginning. It is not easy to define exactly how a poet performs this essential act of creation: it is a matter partly of the manipulation of vowels and consonants—and some of Yeats's most famous poems, such as *Innisfree*, have been analysed to show his astonishing mastery of this side of his craft; it is also partly a matter of the rhythms that are woven across the regular metrical beat of the line, which give such individuality to the ear that a quatrain of four-beat lines by Yeats could never be mistaken for one by Blake, or Hopkins, or Eliot; equally important is the choice of vocabulary, the extent to which archaic or poetic words are associated with more current or colloquial words, latinate words with Anglo-Saxon words, monosyllables with polysyllables. Look, for instance, at the way he introduces a truculent word like 'supersession' into one of his shortest and best-known poems:

Nor dread nor hope attend
A dying animal;
A man awaits his end
Dreading and hoping all;
Many times he died,
Many times rose again.
A great man in his pride
Confronting murderous men
Casts derision upon
Supersession of breath;
He knows death to the bone——
Man has created death.

In all these things, Yeats very rapidly established his own, immediately identifiable manner, and though his skill increased as he grew older—if we except perhaps a period just before the 1914 war when he seemed to be marking time—it is the same quality that attracts us in the last poems he wrote as in *The Sorrow of Love* or *The Song of the Wandering Aengus.* He was particularly successful in overcoming what seems to be the chief stumbling-block of so many modern poets, the assimilation of the technical and apparently unpoetical word into his verse; and as he began to drop the 'embroideries out of old mythologies' and turn more and more to the concrete world of contemporary Ireland, he showed that he did not have to limit his range, as an exquisite minor poet like Ernest Dowson did in his own generation, in order to avoid producing the lumpy and indigestible porridge that has been offered so often and so hopefully in the last twenty years in the guise of honeydew and milk of Paradise.

He transfigured the colloquial, as Eliot has in his own very different way. The *Meditation in Time of Civil War* provides many examples of this power of his, none more striking than the section called 'The Road at My Door':

> An affable irregular
> A heavily built Falstaffian man,
> Comes cracking jokes of civil war
> As though to die by gunshot were
> The finest play under the sun. . . .

And who but Yeats could have succeeded in that opening section of the poem called *Ancestral Houses*, which is conceived in the grand manner if ever a poem was, in concluding a stanza so easily, so conversationally, as with the lines:

> And maybe the great-grandson of that house,
> For all its bronze and marble's but a mouse.

All these elements that I have separated from Yeats's craftsmanship, the way vowels and consonants are handled, the counterpointing and cross-rhythms, the choice and mixture of vocabulary, are, I think, important in the final make-up of his individual music; but the *Meditation in Time of Civil War* brings us up against what was, in his later manner at least, the supreme secret of style: I can only call it the tone of voice. It derives from all of them, but it is at the same time something more than their sum total, a quality as elusive as the quality which makes one man a brilliant speaker in public or on the air, and another, of otherwise equal—or greater—gifts, a failure; the final endowment which decides whether posterity will cherish a poet, or not. I do not believe it can be analysed any more than any of the other supreme secrets of genius, though even the most cunning imitator will immediately reveal that he has not got it. It is almost the whole secret of those terse little gnomic poems which Yeats delighted in as he grew older, the culminating example being the *Words for Music Perhaps*, whose creation, after a long illness, Yeats has described himself in that memorable passage of the notes to his *Collected Poems*: 'Then in the spring of 1929 life returned as an impression of the uncontrollable energy and daring of the great creators; it seemed that but for journalism and criticism, all that evasion and explanation, the world would be torn in pieces.'

One of the most precious gifts of the greatest poets has always been their power of concentrated expression: of making even quite a short lyric or ode carry as much 'criticism of life', or imaginative refinement of experience, as a prose-writer can often pack into a novel or a playwright into the three acts of an evening performance, so that through one particular experience or set of images a great range of other experiences is suggested and a few dozen lines seem to extend this radiation almost infinitely. If I were asked whether I should feel more deprived and starved of spiritual food by the loss of the hundred best novels I could name or the hundred best poems, I would unhesitatingly reply that I could more easily spare the novels. And among the hundred poems, I would certainly include several examples from the poetry of our own time, which have just this density and power of radiation, and from Yeats's last period among the first. What is so amazing is that this 'sixty-year-old smiling public man' as he described himself in *Among Schoolchildren*, could write poems of such imaginative splendour and intellectual richness as *Coole and Ballylee, Byzantium, Sailing to Byzantium, The Second Coming* and *Meru*, transforming his early myth-making magic with a magic more completely his own and even more potent after a lifetime of consistent integrity and achievement, so that the poet who has cast off the old mythologies and learnt to walk naked appears at the end in the new, less fancifully but even more superbly embroidered robes of the prophet-philosopher. We may discount much of the neo-platonism and the hints of the occult, as we may discount much of the speculation on time in T. S. Eliot's later work, but the residue of visionary poetry is so tremendous that we can easily accept the playing with theories as the necessary scaffolding for a mind which had long before rejected conventional religion, and whose work derives much of its intensity from the search for a substitute—from the attempt to make high poetry itself take its place:

> Another emblem there! That stormy white
> But seems a concentration of the sky;
> And, like the soul, it sails into the sight
> And in the morning's gone, no man knows why;
> And is so lovely that it sets to right
> What knowledge or its lack had set awry,
> So arrogantly pure, a child might think
> It can be murdered with a spot of ink. . . .

It may be that, almost unconsciously, today's generation is fascinated by the aristocratic note in Yeats's poetry, that quality in his make-up which brought him to his well-known eccentric political sympathies, but represents something that is rapidly vanishing from our world and is regretted ever more deeply as it vanishes; nevertheless, it is, I think, finally, the prophetic and visionary power of his last work that completes his sway over the poets who have followed him. And as civilization staggers, as in the climax of a drunken dance, from the rape of Poland to Belsen, and from Belsen to Hiroshima, and so on to the unimaginable horrors of the future, Yeats's famous vision of the 'rough beast' that 'slouches towards Bethlehem to be born' while

> Turning and turning in the widening gyre
> The falcon cannot hear the falconer;
> Things fall apart, the centre cannot hold. . . .

with its wonderful catching-up and modulation of Shelley's words in *Prometheus Unbound*, can only appear more and more ominously apposite to an appalled world that seems incapable of averting the birth. And the sibylline master does not only see what is swelling in the womb of time more truly than all the politicians, economists and Frankenstein-fiddlers in their laboratories, but admits us also for dazzling moments into that air of eternity, the gates of which only poets can unlock, when we know that civilization, our civilization like all those which have preceded it

> . . . is hooped together, brought
> Under a rule, under the semblance of peace
> By manifold illusion, but man's life is thought
> And he, despite its terror, cannot cease
> Ravening, raging and uprooting that he may come
> Into the desolation of reality:
> Egypt and Greece good-bye, and good-bye Rome.

Virginia Woolf

When I think of Virginia Woolf, the picture that first springs to my mind is of her workroom in Tavistock Square. It was a big, square studio with a skylight, built on to the basement. It was used by the Hogarth Press as a stock room, and there in the midst of an ever-encroaching forest of books was her desk, stuffed and littered with papers, letters and innumerable half-finished manuscripts. I was learning my job as manager then, in the little back room, and she would pass my window every day as she went in to her work. She would stay there for hours, writing steadily; if it wasn't a novel, it was an article, or a story, or her own diary; I don't think she was happy unless her pen was moving over the paper in that thin, elegant, intellectual handwriting with the beautiful flourishes; and that is the reason why, after her death, so many unknown treasures were found among her papers, though only too few were in a finished state. Sometimes she would move over to the disused scullery that had been converted by Leonard Woolf into a printing room, and help to set up type for the occasional small volumes that were still produced entirely by the Hogarth Press; and sometimes, when a new book had just been published and there was a heavy rush of orders to be dealt with, she would come into the front room and work with the staff, tying up parcels and sticking on labels. The young poets and novelists who came to leave manuscripts, hoping desperately that the so famous, elusive author would read and approve their works, never guessed that she was there in person, working unobtrusively under their very eyes.

The other picture that comes continually to my mind is of evenings down at Monk's House, the old cottage in Sussex, which she and Leonard Woolf had bought and rebuilt for themselves. After dinner, in the room on the first floor that looked out on the little garden with its orchard on one side and goldfish pond on the other, she would sit in her chair by the fire, smoking in a long holder the strong cigarettes she rolled for herself, and talk. She wanted to know about everybody and everything. What was young X writing? Was it true that so-and-so had broken up his best friend's marriage? What did we think of the latest magazine? The latest production of *The Duchess of Malfi* or *Twelfth Night*? What on earth was she to answer to the old bore Z, who kept on writing her pompous fan letters from America? She delighted in witty gossip, and would discuss the comic and tragic events of the day as keenly as the deepest problems of literature. There can never have been anyone on whom the mantle of acknowledged literary greatness lay less heavily.

Above all, until the very end of her life, she maintained her interest in what young people were writing. She did a great deal of reading for the Hogarth Press, and, except for specialist works on economic or political problems, there were few manuscripts submitted to us which did not pass through her hands. She was always on the lookout for promise, for a sign of the true gift; and on the last occasion I saw her, only a week or two before her death, she discussed a first collection of poems sent in by a young writer. There was much she did not like about them, she found them too often obscure and confusing, but, nevertheless, there were moments of music, flashes of imagery, that made her feel he ought to be published. She took away with her a bundle of stories and poems which had been submitted to *New Writing*, and her wise and sympathetic comments on them—comments for which she apologized, feeling she was not up to her best—reached me only shortly before the news of the tragedy.

Her attitude towards the writing of the generation below her was of a piece with her whole attitude towards literature. One may think that she failed sometimes in appreciation, but the remarkable thing is how quickly, most of the time, she grasped the changing conditions and changing outlook on life that lay beneath a change of taste, and how finely she could distinguish the dross from the gold in what was new. This emerges clearly from two articles she wrote about the work of my own contemporaries, the

Letter to a Young Poet and *The Leaning Tower*. She was critical of many inadequacies, but with her fresh insight and intelligence she saw why the inadequacies were there, the generous impulse and the fatal setting which prevented the birth of the great work of art. But while she recognized the difficulties, and all the claims of the contemporary, she distrusted the clamour of opposing 'schools' and 'movements', and gave sound reasons for her distrust. 'Never think yourself singular,' she says in the *Letter to a Young Poet*, 'never think your own case much harder than other people's.' She suggests that it is the enormous development of the reading public that encourages the idea that literature is full of violent battles, victories and defeats.

Now of course writers themselves know very well that there is not a word of truth in all this—there are no battles, and no murders, and no defeats, and no victories. But as it is of the utmost importance that readers should be amused, writers acquiesce. They dress themselves up. They act their parts; one leads; the other follows. One is romantic, the other realist. One is advanced, the other out of date. There is no harm in it, so long as you take it as a joke, but once you believe in it, once you begin to take yourself seriously as a leader or as a follower, as a modern or as a conservative, then you become a self-conscious, biting and scratching little animal whose work is not of the slightest value or importance to anybody. Think of yourself rather as something much humbler and less spectacular, but to my mind far more interesting—a poet in whom live all the poets of the past, from whom all poets in time to come will spring . . . in short you are an immensely ancient, complex and continuous character, for which reason please treat yourself with respect. . . .

Always this idea of the immense antiquity of literature, the enduring tradition, dominated her critical thinking. Readers who know her chiefly through her novels are apt to think of her only as a daring innovator in style and manner, the truly modern writer who had finally broken with the conventions of the pre-1914 novel. She was indeed very conscious of the chasm that the First World War had opened up across the life of her time, and of the demands this difference made on the artist who would interpret it, but her greatness was to combine with this awareness an understanding of the achievement of the past, towering always on the horizon, warning and inspiring and restoring a sense of proportion to all who were sensible enough to lift their eyes to it. The range of intellectual interests revealed in her first collection of essays, *The Common Reader*, is sufficient proof of this: Chaucer, Elizabethan plays, Defoe, Jane Austen, Montaigne, the Russian novelists, Joseph Conrad are among her subjects, and she treats them all with the same mixture of finely discriminating intelligence and common sense, the same loving, recreating force of imagination. The intensity of her sympathy varies; she has a bias towards the feminine, being herself a determined feminist, and also towards the great diary and memoir writers; but her passionate belief in literature and her sense of its wholeness were always there in the background. At the end of the last essay in the volume, *How it Strikes a Contemporary*, she writes:

> As for the critics, whose task it is to pass judgment upon the books of the moment, whose work, let us admit, is difficult, dangerous, and often distasteful, let us ask them to be generous of encouragement, but sparing of those wreaths and coronets which are so apt to get awry, and fade, and make the wearers, in six months' time, look a little ridiculous. Let them take a wider, a less personal view of modern literature, and look indeed upon the writers as if they were engaged upon some vast building, which being built by common effort, the separate workmen may well remain anonymous. . . . Let me recall to their memory that gaunt aristocrat, Lady Hester Stanhope, who kept a milk-white horse in her stable in readiness for the Messiah, and was for ever scanning the mountain-tops, impatiently but with confidence, for signs of his approach, and ask them to follow her example; scan the horizon; see the past in relation to the future; and so prepare the way for masterpieces to come.

In the same volume, Virginia Woolf reprinted her famous essay on *Modern Fiction*, which originally appeared in 1919 and was in a sense an apologia for the direction her own work was about to take. The change was indeed startling. With her first book, *The Voyage Out*, which was published in 1915 after she had rewritten it from beginning to end at least five times, she is playing the established rules of the game. The handling of the material, the telling of the story disturb no conventional notions; no one could say, 'But I don't understand what she's getting at', as so many bewildered library subscribers were to exclaim to one another later on; the book was only lifted above the average readable novel of the day by a sensibility, an imaginative tone, and a distinction of style that are rare in any novel, let alone a first effort. *Night and Day*, published a year or two later, is in some ways even more conventional. Then came the little volume of short pieces—to call them stories or sketches is to define them too narrowly—called *Monday or Tuesday*; one suddenly finds oneself in an entirely different world. It is no longer the world of solid character and narration, but of suggestion, atmosphere, exquisitely rendered, disembodied moods, glittering descriptions of colour and light, behind the tension of which one can feel an agonized apprehension of beauty and suffering; it is poetry. And from that moment onwards Virginia Woolf was to remain more poet than novelist, forever searching for new means of dissolving prose into poetry, of refining away all but the husk of action in works which still went under the name of novels, and irradiating them with this strange new light.

The intellectual basis for this profound disturbance in her own spirit, she elaborated skilfully in *Modern Fiction* by a destructive critique of three dominant figures in the fiction of the day, Galsworthy, Bennett and Wells, and an appeal to the Russians: 'If we want understanding of the soul and heart where else shall we find it of comparable profundity? If we are sick of our own materialism the least considerable of their novelists has by right of birth a natural reverence for the human spirit.' Hardy, Conrad and Hudson, she claimed, had the root of the matter in them; but she would go further herself:

Admitting the vagueness which afflicts all criticism of novels, let us hazard the opinion that for us at this moment the form of fiction most in vogue more often misses than secures the thing we seek. Whether we call it life or spirit, truth or reality, this the essential thing, has moved off, or on, and refuses to be contained any longer in such ill-fitting vestments as we provide. So much of the enormous labour of proving the solidity, the likeness to life, of the story, is not merely labour thrown away but labour misplaced to the extent of obscuring and blotting out the light of the conception. . . . Examine for a moment an ordinary mind on an ordinary day. The mind receives a myriad impressions—trivial, fantastic, evanescent, or engraved with the sharpness of steel. From all sides they come, an incessant shower of innumerable atoms, and as they fall, as they shape themselves into the life of Monday or Tuesday, the accent falls differently from of old. . . . Life is not a series of gig-lamps symmetrically arranged; life is a luminous halo, a semi-transparent envelope surrounding us from the beginning of consciousness to the end. Is it not the task of the novelist to convey this varying, this unknown and uncircumscribed spirit, whatever aberration or complexity it may display, with as little mixture of the alien and external as possible?

There could be no clearer signpost than these sentences to the great series of novel-poems which were to begin with *Jacob's Room* in 1922 and go on to the wonderful, unrevised *Between the Acts* published after her death in 1941, and on which the fame of Virginia Woolf in the world of letters must ultimately rest. Here, within this 'luminous halo', she attempted again and again to find symbols for human existence; to construct scenes, to weave patterns of imagery and feeling which would contain something of the vision that seemed always to be escaping before it had been fully apprehended; a dazzling vision which had changed the whole course of her art and threatened to crack the walls of her being every time she set out to recapture it. Again and again in these books she introduces characters who are struggling to express the inexpressible, whose intellect or imagination is taut with the effort to reach beyond the frontiers of what has already been discovered or created—images, in many guises, of the artist herself. There are the figures representing the intellect: Jacob pursuing his argument with Timmy Durrant, 'when only half a sentence followed but these half-sentences are like flags set on tops of buildings to the observer of external sights down below'; Mr. Ramsay in *To the Lighthouse*, the philosopher who has got as far as 'Q' in the alphabet of thought, in which 'Z' is only reached once by one man in a generation, bracing himself to reach 'R' and dreading failure as 'a shutter, like the leathern eyelid of a lizard, flickered over the intensity of his gaze and obscured the letter "R"'. This dread of failure in the attempt is always near her chosen characters. It oppresses Lily Briscoe in *To the Lighthouse* until the very end when she suddenly sees how to finish her picture. It is a raging despair in Miss La Trobe, the mysterious producer of the pageant in *Between The Acts*, who groans 'A failure?!', as she puts away the records and crosses the terrace where 'she had suffered triumph, humiliation, ecstasy, despair—for nothing', to find her ultimate vision dawning on her at last in the village pub. It breaks in for a moment on the apparent triumph of Mrs. Dalloway, who has created not a pageant but a party, causing her inwardly to cry, 'Why, after all, did she do these things? Why seek pinnacles and stand drenched in fire? Might it consume her anyhow! Burn her to cinders!' Beside the male thinkers and the artists, the arrangers, are the poets and visionaries: Neville, for instance, in *The Waves*, whose 'roots go down through veins of lead and silver', and who describes himself: 'sealed and blind, with earth stopping my ears, I have yet heard rumour of wars; and the nightingale; have felt the hurrying of many troops of men flocking hither and thither in quest of civilization like flocks of birds migrating seeking the summer.' Isa, in *Between the Acts*, is lost to her real surroundings as she muses in the garden: 'Where do I wander? Down what draughty tunnels? Where the eyeless wind blows? And there grows nothing for the eye. No roses. To issue where? In some harvestless dim field where no evening lets fall her mantle; nor sun rises. All's equal there. Unblowing, ungrowing are the roses there. Change is not; nor the mutable and lovable; nor greetings nor partings; nor furtive findings and feelings, where hand seeks hand and eye seeks shelter from the eye?' Neville experiences the sensation, part pain and part relief, of returning to the 'machine' of everyday life from his explorations into the poetic; from the blinding, prophetic hallucinations of the shell-shocked Septimus Warren Smith in *Mrs. Dalloway*, the descent to the normal is more terrifying, but Lucretia, his wife, finds in his poems and scribblings something not altogether madness. Like Rhoda in *The Waves*, Mrs. Jarvis in *Jacob's Room* is troubled in her moments of vision by something incommunicable, something unfulfilled. 'Yes, yes, when the lark soars; when the sheep, moving a step or two onwards, crop the turf, and at the same time set their bells tinkling; when the breeze first blows, then dies down, leaving the cheek kissed; when the ships on the sea below seem to cross each other and pass on as if drawn by an invisible hand; when there are distant concussions in the air and phantom horsemen galloping, ceasing; when the horizon swims blue, green, emotional—then Mrs. Jarvis, heaving a sigh, thinks to herself, "If only someone could give me. . . . If I could give someone. . . ." '

For these successive expeditions towards the inexpressible, Virginia Woolf never chooses quite the same road, never uses quite the same technique. Interior monologue is the main instrument, appearing in all the novels, ranging from the most mundane reflections to the pure poetry of Isa, fluid and informal in all but *The Waves* where it becomes static and formal, but used a little differently in each. In *Jacob's Room* an extreme impressionism covers many years and many different scenes by the slightest touches—a paragraph of description, or a few thoughts, or a burst of dialogue is often enough for each; with *Mrs. Dalloway* the events and reflections of a single day fill a book of much the same length; in *To the Lighthouse* two scenes of fairly short duration in time are divided by a choral passage of description, *Time Passes*, in which time moves infinitely faster and actual events are only indicated here and there in brief bracketed sentences. With *The Waves* the technique is more radically altered, but is nevertheless a logical possible development from the earlier techniques; the new form of the interior dialogue is only more deliberate and artificial, and an attempt is made to present it as if it were not 'interior' at all, but spoken, as it were, dramatically; the choral interludes where the waves break on the shore and the sun slowly crosses the heavens to mark the passage of years are the development of devices already experimented with in *Jacob's Room* and *To The Lighthouse*. The problem in each of these books is the problem which lay concealed all the time beneath the endeavour to leave out plot, and concentrate on 'the soul': how shall one show the workings of time on the lives of people? On each occasion she found a new solution, but the curious structural uncertainty of her next novel, *The Years*, makes one feel that she became increasingly dissatisfied with these solutions. *Between the Acts* to some extent avoids the problem; one cannot tell from it whether a new solution was emerging in her mind at the time of her death.

It is perhaps impossible to analyse all that gives these works their entirely unique and haunting quality, that makes one feel that nowhere in the English novel have such profound things been said about human existence, and by the slightest means. One can only distinguish some of the main elements in Virginia Woolf's art. Above all, her astonishing sense of form and rhythmic pulse. *Jacob's Room* seems to describe a perfect parabola, from the opening when the cry of Archer is heard calling for Jacob whom he cannot find on the beach, to the cry wrung out of Bonamy at the end for the Jacob he will never find again; and the end of *To the Lighthouse* seems to resolve all the themes of the book without one note wrong; it is as if one were listening to a flawlessly written piece of music and the emotional and intellectual satisfaction at the end is complete—though it must remain in the symbolism of the journey to the lighthouse and escapes any attempt at rational definition. There are themes which recur again and again, from novel to novel. The cry of 'Jacob! Jacob!' that rises from *Jacob's Room* is echoed by the cry of 'Mrs. Ramsay! Mrs. Ramsay!' from Lily Briscoe in *To the Lighthouse*, notes of an almost unendurable sadness that sounds softer or more poignant through all the books. It is round this sadness, this longing for something that cannot be reached or found again, that *The Waves* is constructed, where Percival who died in India repeats the theme of Jacob, the young man like a Greek statue come to life. The echoing sadness, and the continual questioning of life and death which accompanies it, are often deepened by the introduction and repetition of lines of poetry, 'O, western wind, when wilt thou blow', for instance, in *The Waves*, and 'Luriana Lurilee' in *To the Lighthouse*. The poets themselves are always present, Shakespeare, Shelley, Byron, the Greeks, their names appear again and again, and each time it is as if lamps were being lit; civilization, what man has created with art and learning—and with love—appears always as a light against darkness; Cambridge is imagined as emitting a radiance into the day as well as the night; in *To the Lighthouse* the *Boeuf en daube* dinner, with darkness creeping up to the window panes becomes, as if by magic, no longer a dinner but an image of all this. Greece is one symbol among many she uses to create a sense of the past spreading illimitably round the lives of her characters; there are the strange skulls and bleached bones, the Phoenicians sleeping in the barrows, the old Barn like a Greek temple, the banners trembling above tombs. This sense of the past blends with the sea, the sound of waves breaking on the shore which is heard not only in *The Waves* but in *Jacob's Room* and *To the Lighthouse* as well; and when the pulse of time is not sounding from the sea it falls from clock-towers, in *Mrs. Dalloway* and *Between the Acts*, when the hour booms out over city or countryside. The past and its mystery; death and its mystery; love with its mystery, now transforming the whole of life with its glow, now savage as tigers; the dazzling surface radiance of the world and a terror and despair lurking always beneath; nowhere in modern writing have these things found symbols more audacious and memorable than in the novel-poems of Virginia Woolf, so that one can truly say that she enlarged the sensibility of her time, and *changed* English literature.

The strain was terrific, what she suffered in this giving birth to masterpieces not to be measured. When a novel was reaching its completion, she would often have to leave it altogether, not once but several times, and go away or rest in the writing of lighter sketches and reviews. She took other longer holidays; she wrote *Flush*, and *Orlando*, and *A Room of One's Own*, and thereby gained a delighted reading public that was to be checked and baffled when the next novel appeared. She also showed that she could write a long biography with all the skill, tact, and understanding she displayed in her shorter portraits; *Roger Fry*, most of which was written during the war, is a model of how to write the life of a contemporary figure who had also been a close friend. But at the same time as *Roger Fry* she was also working on the last posthumously published novel, *Between the Acts*. This was the answer to those who believed that Virginia Woolf had exhausted the poet in her; it never received her final shaping, and rough corners stick out of it here and there; nevertheless, as it stands, it must be considered one of her greatest, most poetic achievements. Beneath this slight story of a pageant which takes place in an English village in the late summer of 1939 lies a parable, a vision of the whole of English history which reaches out to becoming a vision of the whole of life. The poetic symbolism is as subtle and profound as ever, more frightening perhaps than in any of her earlier books. Instead of a fully realized picture she gives us a series of brilliant, suggestive moments, stabs of paint of a startling beauty on a canvas in which she seems to leave large spaces empty. It is possible that if she had lived she might have filled in those gaps and elaborated the symbolism; but she may have felt, on this last and most daring of her voyages of exploration towards the inexpressible, that these hints and unfinished outlines were all she trusted herself to put on her map of the territory she was discovering. The imminence of the war is only directly indicated by the bombers that suddenly roar over the pageant drowning the speaker's words for a few seconds. Yet it is there all through. It is as if she were trying to say that though the moment of time in which we live may seem so violent that it reduces us to 'scraps, orts and fragments', and the pattern of history to meaninglessness, nevertheless even this moment is part of a great developing process which has brought so many changes already, that there is a unity, a single process which we may fail, in our agony of action and suffering, to discern. The note of sadness, the questioning run through *Between the Acts* as they run through the earlier novels; but there is gaiety too, and the final impression is of hope and confidence, more marked perhaps than ever before. The closing pages, in which the particular place and the particular time seem to disappear are, surely, an affirmation of belief that there has always been struggle 'in the heart of darkness in the fields of night', before a new life could be born, that over our present troubles the creative forces of life will, once again as so often in the past, triumph as inevitably as the day follows night.

It was not the war which brought Virginia Woolf to the tragedy which ended her life; in the great crisis of 1940 she showed an imperturbability in the face of disaster and personal danger that would have been remarkable among many of her far less sensitive compatriots. No, it was the strain of the task she had set herself, the dread of the fine instrument, which had created so many wonderful things already, breaking under the pressure of this last, heroic attempt. One cannot help thinking of Rhoda in *The Waves*, who cries: 'There is some check in the flow of my being; a deep stream presses on some obstacle; it jerks; it tugs; some knot in the centre resists. Oh, this is pain, this is anguish! I faint, I fail. Now my body thaws: I am unsealed, I am incandescent. Now the stream pours in a deep tide, fertilizing, opening the shut, forcing the tight-folded, flooding free. To whom shall I give all that now flows through me, from my warm, my porous body? I will gather my flowers and present them—Oh! to whom?' At the end that 'knot in the centre' resisted too inexorably, and she gave her garland of flowers to—Death. What she might have achieved if that marvellous and still unstanched flow had broken down the 'check' once more, one can only guess; the full richness and significance of what she had already given the world is yet to be understood.

The Life of the Prodigal Son

At one time in my life I wanted to write poetry above all things, and I went to Vienna to devote myself to it. I don't quite know why I chose Vienna—I am sure the reasons I gave myself and others at the time only partly expressed the truth—but it seems to me now that I was drawn on by obscure impressions of childhood, things told me or overheard by me or seen in picture books, and sustained by the thought that I should be absolutely alone. And one of the few books I took with me, perhaps the one I was most careful to pack, was an English translation of Rilke's *Notebook of Malte Laurids Brigge*.

It was not my first acquaintance with this extraordinary book, which I now think one of the most original and beautiful books of the twentieth century; I had already, at various times, dipped into it, and I had already fallen under the spell of Rilke's poetry that has worked so powerfully on my generation; but I was now going to immerse myself in it under the conditions in which it demands to be read: in solitude, in a strange city, and with poetry in my head. It stayed with me, my favourite reading, all that late summer and autumn. Much of it I found hermetic, even incomprehensible, and impossible to relate to any central pattern; for it demands not only some knowledge of Rilke's own life to explain its riddles, but also a marriage of experiences and conceptions of which I was still too young to be aware. Again and again, however, I came upon passages that enthralled and haunted me, and one passage in particular that I read and re-read and tried to absorb into myself with all my assimilative power of mind, the passage in which Malte describes how to be a poet:

> Verses amount to so little when one begins to write them young. One ought to wait and gather sense and sweetness a whole life long, and a long life if possible, and then, quite at the end, one might perhaps be

able to write ten good lines. For verses are not, as people imagine, simply feelings (we have these soon enough); they are experiences. In order to write a single verse, one must see many cities, and men and things; one must get to know animals and the flight of birds, and the gestures that the little flowers make when they open out in the morning. One must be able to return in thought to roads in unknown regions, to unexpected encounters, and to partings that had been long foreseen; to days of childhood that are still indistinct, and to parents whom one had to hurt when they sought to give one some pleasure which one did not understand (it would have been a pleasure to someone else); to childhood's illnesses that so strangely begin with such a number of profound and grave transformations, to days spent in rooms withdrawn and quiet, and to mornings by the sea, to the sea itself, to oceans, to nights of travel that rushed along loftily and flew with all the stars—and still it is not enough to be able to think of all this. There must be memories of many nights of love, each one unlike the others, of the screams of women in labour, and of women in childbed, light and blanched and sleeping, shutting themselves in. But one must also have been beside the dying, must have sat beside the dead in a room with open windows and with fitful noises. And still it is not enough yet to have memories. One must be able to forget them when they are many, and one must have the immense patience to wait until they come again. For it is the memories themselves that matter. Only when they have turned to blood within us, to glance and gesture, nameless and no longer to be distinguished from ourselves—only then can it happen that in a most rare hour the first word of a poem arises in their midst and goes forth from them.

This seemed to me then one of the most wonderful releasing statements about poetry that I had ever read. It is, I can now see, an ideal which might lead to the writing of a great deal of very bad poetry, unless corrected by what one might call the *grammarian's* attitude which had been in fashion in the circles I moved in at Cambridge and directly after: the view that the first essential for the poet is to be able to think clearly and to use words precisely, and to express a certain intellectual energy in his views by his *wit*, in the sense of the term defined by T. S. Eliot. If the ultra-romantic view was responsible for a great deal of showy nonsense, this grammarian's view, admirable in its due place and proportion, was in danger, if slavishly followed, of producing mere arid exercises, the purely masculine without that feminine and intuitive element which is essential to poetry; all the more arid and marginal if the poet had also come under the influence of the equally fashionable 'clinical' view, which insisted that poetry was the resolution in words of obscure psychological tensions in the mind of its author. Rilke's words, so eloquent, so simple and so evocative, avoiding so carefully the exalted peaks of the claims made by the great romantics such as Shelley, seemed to me to present exactly what was missing in these views; a vision of how poetry was created or should be created in our post-romantic age, not by taking great themes and giving them the noblest treatment one was capable of, but by allowing the whole of experience, of years of thought and feeling and observation to be distilled in the depth of one's imagination, unforced and unhurried, to form their precious fluid. And, above all, it presented a design for the dedicated life a poet should lead, not merely for his working hours but for the whole preparation of himself before and between those (perhaps very brief) periods.

This ideal, of a life devoted to poetry, planned to provide the opportunity for every kind of experience that might nurture the poetic being and avoid every experience and entanglement that might be destructive to it, was grand enough when Rilke wrote the *Notebook* before the first world war. It is grander, in fact it is heroic now, when the wars and revolutions of our age have destroyed the old Europe, in which leisure was possible even if only for the more fortunate classes and those to whom they acted as patrons, and when the cancerous development of state control and interference has created an environment where everything conspires to ruin the inner life.

The fulfilment of the inner life was Rilke's own supreme object, and the passion with which he endowed Malte. Almost the last words in the *Notebook* are:

> Long ago he had detached himself from the accidents of fate to which men cling, but now even whatever of pleasure and pain were necessary lost their spicy after taste and became pure and nourishing to him. From the roots of his being there sprang the sturdy, evergreen plant of a fertile joy. He was wholly engrossed in learning to handle what constituted his inner life; he wanted to omit nothing, for he doubted not that his love dwelt and grew in all this. Indeed, his inward serenity went so far that he resolved to overtake the most important of those things which he had hitherto been unable to accomplish, the things he had simply allowed to slip past while he waited.

The *Notebook* itself can be described as the record of how Rilke learnt, in the first period of his life as a poet, to 'handle his inner life'; it is a distillation of experience, through the invented character of the young Danish poet, that follows remarkably faithfully the prescription for a poet's life Rilke gives within it. All the wanderings, both over Europe and inside his own world of thought, all the emotions and spiritual struggles, all the provocative outward events and inward imaginative discoveries of six years of Rilke's life are mirrored in Malte's notebook; and the history of its development is a fascinating study of his creative processes at work.

We know from Maurice Betz, with whom Rilke collaborated in the French translation of the *Notebook* during his stay in Paris in 1925, that the original germ was Rilke's discovery of a book called *The Diary of a Priest*, by Sigbjorn Obstfelder, a young Norwegian writer who had come to live in Paris and died there at the early age of thirty-two. Rilke read this story of the struggles of a tormented soul to find God, a pursuit that ends in madness, at a time when his enthusiasm for anything Scandinavian was at its height; and the fact that Obstfelder had, like Rilke, been a stranger alone in Paris as a young man, made a special bond of sympathy. Rilke seems to have been haunted by the Norwegian from the beginning: and in the end his imaginative occupation of his life became so intense that he speaks of Malte as if he were a living person, always beside him; who was, as it were, dictating the book. 'I must not advance beyond him and his suffering too far,' he says in a letter to his wife in 1908, 'otherwise I will no longer understand him.' It is always in this strain that he speaks of the book; and his description of the sudden sprouting of the seed that Obstfelder's work had planted in his mind is like the account of a spiritual possession. Maurice Betz reports Rilke as telling him the story as follows:

At that time I was in Rome. I had been living for several months in a little studio which had been lent me in the park of the Villa Strohl-Fern. The Italian spring disappointed me by its undue haste, and my reading of Jacobsen awakened my longing for that Northern country where I knew no one except the good Ellen Key, to whom I had dedicated *The Stories of God*. I wrote a series of dialogues between a young man and a young girl who confide their little secrets to each other. The young man told the girl a great deal about a Danish poet, a certain Malte, whom he had known and who died young in Paris. The girl wanted to know more about Malte, and the young man was indiscreet enough to tell her that his friend had left a diary, while he admitted that he himself had never looked into it yet. The girl begged him to let her see it. I succeeded in keeping her waiting for several days by various subterfuges, but her curiosity increased and in the end she began to build up her own picture of Malte. I realized that it was not permissible for me to offer resistance any longer, and so I interrupted the dialogue and began to write Malte's own diary without troubling any more with the subsidiary personages who had led me to him almost against my will.

From that moment in 1904 the *Notebook* was always in Rilke's mind; and from 1906 to 1910 with occasional intervals of a few weeks or months when Malte's problems became too difficult for him to solve and he had to turn away from the 'heavy, heavy book', it was his major preoccupation as a writer. During that time he was restless and dissatisfied, with frequent breakdowns in health, always moving from one place to another, but experiencing new scenes and making new friends—among them, one of the most important in his whole life, Rodin—the stimulus of which can be traced again and again in the *Notebook*. There was, first of all, the excitement of getting to know Denmark, the country he was to make Malte's own. It is probably true, as Countess Wydenbruck suggests in her book,* that the friends he made during these years among the north German Lutheran nobility, were probably as important, or even more important than his brief experiences of Denmark itself, in providing him with material for building up the background of Malte's family. Nevertheless, the Danish visit was responsible for at least one of the most striking and characteristic passages in the *Notebook*, where the young Malte and his mother visit the family of the Schulius, the great central wing of whose manor-house has recently been burnt down. Rilke describes the arrival by sleigh, in darkness and snowstorm:

One might have imagined one saw the church tower on the left, but suddenly the outline of the park wall appeared, high up, almost on top of us, and we found ourselves in the long avenue. The tinkling of the bells no longer ceased abruptly; it seemed to hang in clusters right and

* *Rilke: Man and Poet*, a book to which I am immensely indebted in the preparation of this study.

left on the trees. Then we swung in and drove around something, passed something else on the right, and came to a halt in the centre.

Georg had quite forgotten that the house was no longer there, and for all of us at that moment it was there. We ascended the front steps that led up to the old terrace, and only wondered at finding all in darkness. Suddenly a door opened below and behind us on the left, and someone cried, 'This way!' at the same time lifting and swinging a dim lantern. My Father laughed: 'We are wandering about here like ghosts,' and he helped us down the steps again.

'But still there was a house there just now,' said Mother. . . .

The actual experience from which this episode was created, is related in a letter to Lou Andreas Salome in December 1904.He describes how he went to visit his Danish friend Ellen Key in a lonely country house that belonged to her brother:

We found ourselves in the courtyard, enclosed by the small lateral wings of the château. But there, where four flights of steps ascended with a great effort from the deep snow of the courtyard to the terrace, on which a balustrade with ornamental vases appeared to herald the château itself, there was nothing except a few snow-covered shrubs and a grey, glimmering sky, against which I could distinguish snowflakes falling through the twilight. I had to remind myself that the building no longer existed, that I had been told how it had burnt down to the ground years ago, but still I could not help feeling that there must be something there, that the air behind the balustrade was not the same as the air around, but was still divided into passages and rooms and a great central hall, a high, empty, forsaken, twilit hall. . . .

Thus the actual description in the *Notebook* is taken almost exactly from Rilke's own experiences at Oby, but he transforms and enlarges it by making it pass through the wondering mind of a small boy who, quickly taking up the hint dropped by his mother is overcome by the idea of this phantom house, tries to slip away to see it again, and *believes* in it in spite of the laughter of the others: ' "Of course they only go when it is not there," I thought contemptuously; "if Mother and I lived here, it would always be there." Mother looked distraught, while the others were all talking at once. She was certainly thinking of the house.'

Another striking example of Rilke's way of refashioning the experiences of these years to make them part of the *Notebook* is the passage towards the end, where Malte is once more reminded of

Abelone, vividly and with a new insight, by a girl he meets at a salon one afternoon in Venice. The famous description of Venice, not 'the soft, narcotic Venice' that is the illusion of the 'somnolent foreigners', but the real Venice of winter that reveals itself when they have gone, 'awake, brittle to breaking-point, and not in the least dream-like: this Venice willed into being in the midst of nothing and set on sunken forests, created by force, and in the end so thoroughly manifest', 'this inventive state that bartered the salt and glass of its poverty for the treasures of the nations', was directly inspired by the winter he spent in the city in 1907. The same images occur in a letter he wrote to his wife at the time, and in the poem *Spaetherbst in Venedig* which he published in *New Poems*:

> Aber vom Grund aus alten Waldskeletten
> Steigt willen auf: als sollte über Nacht
>
> der General des Meeres die Galeeren
> verdoppeln in dem wachen Arsenal. . . .

Even more fundamental to the purpose of the book was the vision of Paris he conjured up, in the opening passages of the *Notebook*, out of his early experiences when he went there for the first time in 1902, and his later impressions in 1907, when he shut himself up in his room in the Rue Cassette and worked at the *New Poems*, the book on Rodin and the *Notebook* itself throughout the summer and autumn. Again, nothing could be less sentimental than the vision this poet, who has so often been accused of sentimentality, created of Paris: for him it seemed always to be a city of macabre happenings, of suffering and poverty (except when he thought of it as the home of Rodin):

> People come here, then, to live? I should rather have thought that they came here to die. I have been out, and I saw hospitals. I saw a poor fellow stagger and fall. People gathered round him; so I was spared the rest. I saw a pregnant woman. She dragged herself heavily along a high, warm wall, now and again groping for it as if to assure herself it was still there. . . .

These are the opening words of the *Notebook*, and they set the tone for all that comes after. His very first letter to his wife from Paris, in 1902, records the same impression, and shows that

Malte's, that Obstfelder's nightmares had been his own: 'I am appalled at the great number of hospitals here. Legions of sick people, armies of dying men, populations of corpses—I have never felt this as strongly in any other city.' Even the man with St. Vitus's Dance appears first of all as a person actually observed and described in one of his letters a year later. And the macabre episode of the medical student in the room next door, whose eyelid refused to stay open and who in his misery and nervous exhaustion stamped up and down while a noise repeated itself—'the noise made by any round, tin object, such as the lid of a canister, when it slips from one's grasp'—this, too, came directly out of his own experience, while he was working at the *Notebook* in the Rue Cassette.

All these scenes, these moments of intense imaginative apprehension, Rilke was able to work into the fabric of the *Notebook*, while preserving the thematic wholeness of the book, with an art that reveals itself as more consummate with every reading. The method he had chosen, the apparently random record of an intimate journal, allowed him considerable latitude; and as he later admitted to Maurice Betz, his idea of giving it the air of incompleteness that the journal of the dead Obstfelder might well have had, so took possession of him that he did not even collect all the fragments he had written at one time or another for use in it. But the book is one; as a poem of loneliness and suffering, of death in all its mysterious and terrible aspects, the spiritual voyage through a haunted darkness of a young man who strives to recapture the beauty and meaning of his childhood; and to fulfil what he had left there incomplete and unsatisfied, by reliving his memories and using all his maturer powers to understand where and why he had failed to answer all the demands of heart and imagination made on him. The *Notebook* was to Rilke a 'heavy, heavy book', causing him such disturbance and exhaustion of spirit, because it was a delving into his own failures in the inner life; and yet, unlike Malte, he finally surmounted these failures to a miraculous degree by the very fact of writing out Malte's suffering. 'The creative artist is not permitted to select or to turn away from any form of existence,' he wrote in an illuminating letter on Baudelaire's poem *La Charogne* in October 1907, 'surely among his earlier works there must be some where he overcame himself with a mighty effort, right to the utmost limits of love. Beyond this surrender lies saintliness, beginning with small things, the simple existence of a love that has passed the test, and, without boasting, approaches everything.' He was about to make that surrender himself, and the anticipation of it lies in what follows: 'Suddenly (for the first time) I understood Malte Laurids's fate. Is it not that the ordeal was too great for him, that he could not pass the actual test, though he was theoretically convinced of its necessity, so much so that he sought it out instinctively until it haunted him? The book of Malte Laurids once it is written, will be nothing but the story of this insight, exemplified in one for whom it was too mighty. . . .'

It was this insight which drew Malte to the story of the Prodigal Son, which forms part of the great coda to the *Notebook*, and out of which Rilke made one of the most beautiful of his shorter poems. Rilke and Malte then become one in what was perhaps the crucial spiritual problem of the poet's earlier years. 'It will be difficult to persuade me', writes Malte, 'that the story of the Prodigal Son is not the legend of one who did not want to be loved. When he was a child everybody in the house loved him. He grew up knowing nothing else, and as a child he became accustomed to their tenderness. But as a growing boy he sought to lay aside these habits . . . what he then desired was that inner indifference of spirit, which, sometimes, of an early morning in the fields, seized him so unalloyed that he began to run, that he might have neither time nor breath to be more than a transient moment in which the morning became conscious of itself.'

The impulse which, obscurely but so intensely, racks the Prodigal Son, is surely the deep instinct of the artist in one of its many disguises—the artist who must, as he becomes conscious of being an artist, learn to apprehend everything for himself and create his own universe before he can go back to the allegiances and habits of his childhood, so as to be strong enough to treat with them on equal terms. The desire not to be 'more than a transient moment in which the morning becomes conscious of itself' is not unlike Keats's idea that a poet must be capable of being everything and nothing and has no identity, and his confession that 'if a sparrow comes before my window I take part in its existence and pick about the gravel'. The similarity becomes even more striking when Malte goes on to describe, in a passage evidently inspired by Rilke's own holiday in Provence in the spring of 1909, the shepherd's life of the Prodigal Son: 'That was the time which began with his feeling himself a part of the universe and anonymous, like a lingering convalescent. He did not love unless it were that he loved to live. The lowly affection of his sheep did not weigh upon him; like light falling through clouds it dispersed itself about him and gleamed softly on the meadows. In the innocent track of their hunger he strode silently across the pastures of the world. Strangers saw him on the Acropolis; and perhaps he was for a long time one of the shepherds in Les Baux, and saw the petrified age outlast that lofty race which, despite all its acquisition of sevens and threes, could not master the sixteen rays of its star. . . .'

With Rilke, however, the mood of the Prodigal Son was not simply the impulse of the artist to become anonymous; it was at the same time the struggle against loving and being loved, a struggle that had in the end to be abandoned because the complete person, the complete artist (like Baudelaire) learns to love and be loved without shrinking, and the Prodigal Son (not Malte, but Rilke himself) comes home at last. These two themes are introduced in the *Notebook*; but the book is even more than the exploration of the artist's need to lose himself and the Prodigal Son's attempt to escape love, because Rilke's unique poetic faculty makes out of all the gropings within the spirit and journeyings in the outer world, a demonstration of his extraordinary sensibility so vivid and convincing that one feels one has acquired a new kind of perception. One actually sees with him a woman, too suddenly disturbed in her private thoughts, leaving her face in her hands and exposing something flayed and terrible to the onlooker, or one comes to think of death as a being that possesses (has always, in a slow process of growth, possessed) the dying creature and finally enacts its own individual drama—'one *had* it, and that gave one a singular dignity, a quiet pride'. And more than that, with its movement from Malte's own childhood reminiscences, the way of life in the old country houses, to his wanderings in the great cities, and from them to re-creations of legends and famous moments of history, it achieves an evocation of the ancient Europe, a four-dimensional evocation of a haunting resonance and depth. How deliberately this was in Rilke's design, one cannot be sure, but once one has observed how as an artist he loves to present symbols and drop hints within his work of what the work as a whole is fulfilling, one remembers in this connection the picture at the end of the *Notebook* of the sage, the older man who has travelled much in his youth and has long been considered eccentric, as the light burns late in his study:

> He does not always remain bent over his pages; he often leans back and closes his eyes on a line he has read again and again, and its meaning passes into his blood. Never before has he been so certain of the ancient past. He could almost smile at the generations that have mourned it as a lost drama, in which they would have liked to play a part. Now he instantly understands the dynamic significance of that early world-unity, which was something like a new and simultaneous gathering up of all human labour. . . .

In writing the *Notebook* Rilke felt, in a strange way, that he was exploring deeper even than in the poetry he had written hitherto. In his letters we find him talking of going back to the 'discipline of writing verses' and seeking renewal in nature, so that the inner world from the depths of which the *Notebook* was emerging should be 'strengthened and tautened by the influences of the external world'—as if his poetry, compared with his prose, was part of that external world; and in a letter to Rodin, in December 1908, he says, 'In writing poetry one is always helped, and even carried along, by the rhythm of external things—the waters, the winds, the night. But to acquire the rhythms of prose one must go deep down into oneself and find the anonymous and manifold rhythms of the blood.'

It was indeed out of these depths that the *Notebook of Malte Laurids Brigge* was created, and because Rilke was courageous and persistent enough, in spite of illness and misery and the resistance of the wounded memory, to explore them fully, it stands out, ever more clearly as the years go by, as a masterpiece. No book of our time is more passionately dedicated to the inner life, more completely infused with the belief in the primacy of the imagination, of the poetic way of apprehending life; and as the threat to all that it means increases like the deafening roar of a flight of super bombers in the sky, so we instinctively reach out to hold such precious things closer to us.

A Question of Covering One's Tracks

In trying to analyse today the fascination which Henry James's little masterpiece, *The Aspern Papers*, has held for me ever since I first encountered it in my early twenties, I can, I think, distinguish two main elements.

The first is the relation to Shelley, of whose poetry and legend I was even then a devotee. In describing for us the process by which *The Aspern Papers* came to be created, James makes it quite clear that his discovery that Claire Clairmont had been living in Florence when he first visited it, was the germ out of which the story grew. 'The thrill of learning', he says, 'that she had "overlapped", and by so much, and the wonder of my having doubtless at several earlier seasons passed again and again, all unknowing, the door of her house, where she sat above, within call and in her habit as she lived, these things gave me all I wanted; I seem to remember in fact my more or less immediately recognizing that I positively oughtn't—"for anything to come of it"—to have wanted more. I saw, quickly, how something might come of it *thus*; whereas a fine instinct told me that the effect of a nearer view of the case (the case of the overlapping) would probably have had to be quite differently calculable. It was really with another item of knowledge, however, that I measured the mistake I should have made in waking up sooner to the question of opportunity. That item consisted of the action taken on the premises by a person who *had* waked up in time, and the legend of whose consequent adventure, as a few spoken words put it before me, at once kindled a flame. This gentleman, an American of long ago, an ardent Shelleyite, a singularly marked figure and himself in the highest degree a subject for a free sketch—I had known him a little, but there is not a reflected glint of him in *The Aspern Papers*—was named to me as having made interest with Miss Clairmont to be accepted as a lodger on the calculation that she would have Shelley documents for which, in the possibly not remote event of her death, he would then enjoy priority of chance to treat with her representative. He had, at any rate, according to the legend, become on earnest Shelley grounds, her yearning, though also her highly diplomatic *pensionnaire*—but without gathering, as was to befall, the fruit of his design.'

In his own transposition, however, instead of making the mysterious Juliana Bordereau and her poet-lover Europeans, James attempts something that is altogether unusual in his practice: he makes them both cosmopolitan Americans, inventing in Jeffery Aspern a writer of the same Byronic era as Shelley, who had travelled all over Europe and taken deep draughts of its culture, but had remained essentially American. 'That was originally what I had prized him for', admits the 'publishing scoundrel' of *The Aspern Papers*: 'that at a period when our native land was nude and crude and provincial, when the famous "atmosphere" it was supposed to lack was not even missed, when literature was lonely there and art and form almost impossible, he had found means to live and write like one of the first; to be free and general and not at all afraid; to feel, understand and express everything.' He explains the choice of Venice rather than of Florence itself for the scene of the story on the grounds that, for Juliana, 'there were conditions in which she was ideally arrangeable, as happened, especially in respect to the later time and the long undetected survival; there being absolutely no refinement of the mouldy rococo, in human or whatever other form, that you may not disembark at the dislocated water-steps of almost any decayed monument of Venetian greatness in auspicious quest of. It was a question, in fine, of covering one's tracks. . . .'

This was a bold experiment, as James recognized; and he confesses to us that a critical friend (whom he does not name) maintained, apropos not only of *The Aspern Papers* but also of *The Death of the Lion*, *The Figure in the Carpet*, and *The Next Time*, in all of which 'unprecedented and unmatched heroes and martyrs of the artist's ideal' are represented, that such experiments were foredoomed to failure because genius is so strange and astonishing to us that we simply cannot accept it unless in the actual conditions and at the exact time we know it to have appeared. James is unwilling to admit this argument as conclusive, and not unnaturally so, seeing that his attempts were brilliant and approached as near to success as anyone's ever have; but the fact remains that in *The Aspern Papers* the experiment was not successful, at any rate for a European. Who, born on this side of the Atlantic, can read the story without feeling all the time, behind and enveloping the imagined episodes, the romance of Shelley, the Shelley of *Julian and Maddalo* who came to Venice to plead with Byron for Allegra, the daughter of Byron himself and Juliana Bordereau's prototype Claire Clairmont? Certainly each time I have read it, it is of Shelley and Claire that I have thought; and the tension of the story has been created for me by the thought of the excitement I myself would have felt, if I had been so close to a discovery of unknown papers which would have told me more about the intimate joys and sufferings of the actual author of certain known masterpieces of lyric poetry, and not the fictitious American whose poetic triumphs existed only in Henry James's head. And I cannot help thinking that James knew this, intuitively at least, and that the reasons he gives, which I have quoted above, for the choice of Venice were not the only ones: imagine how much the story would lose in enchantment if it took place in a city of Italy which Shelley had not visited.

I am not, of course, suggesting for a moment that my objection to Aspern rests simply on the fact that James made him an American rather than a European, daring as the fancy is that such an American could have existed at such a time; indeed the invention has a certain special attraction of its own for me, because one of the tracks which James, it seems to me, may well have been covering up in the story, is a projection of himself into Aspern. He admits that when he pictured Aspern's home background, it was New York, his own city, that came to him; that the age of Byron and Shelley was the period in the past which held most glamour for him, and in which therefore he would most happily have lived; and that he felt absolute confidence in the reality of Aspern, a reality of which he could have convinced even his critical friend if the limits of the story had not been such as to prevent his giving the character greater body. Aspern, we remember, had 'uncontestably been enriched' by his experiences of Europe, as James had been, though at the same time his muse had remained 'essentially American' as James hoped and believed that his had; would it not be a pardonable exercise of author's vanity if he had allowed himself to dream that long before 'the general transfusion', in an age when the obstacles were far greater, he, like Aspern, would have been able 'to be free and general and not at all afraid; to feel, understand, and express everything?' But if Aspern is partly Henry James, the teller of the story,—the 'publishing scoundrel'—is also partly Henry James, both for a number of touches in the narrative itself and a number of hints in James's observations on it; and while the one is presented as more divinely inspired and more romantic than James knew himself to be, the other is more of a bounder, more callous in his determination to get hold of the coveted papers than James could ever have been. This is not the combination typical of James's imagination, where the open and more or less innocent American is contrasted with the subtle, mysterious and often corrupt European; even Miss Bordereau, who may qualify for such a description, is by origin at least an American, and her rapacity is more excusable than the other's crude subterfuges and dishonesty. And it is just this rather curious variation on his usual pattern that lends strength, in my own view, to the supposition that in creating these two characters James was, perhaps not altogether consciously, dividing his personality between them, making of them his own Dr. Jekyll and Mr. Hyde.

In his article on *The Ambiguity of Henry James*, the American critic Edmund Wilson builds up an interesting and plausible hypothesis about the development of James's art in relation to the themes of love and sex. He believes that one of the reasons why James was increasingly failing to hold his public in the period just before he turned to play-writing, was because there was no consummated love-affair in his novels, and 'you cannot long hold an audience with stories about men wooing women in which the parties either never get together or are never seen as really functioning as lovers'. James was certainly aware that something was wrong, and tried with the plays to create a more intense interest that would compensate for the element the public felt to be missing in the fiction.

The attempt, after five years of effort and anxiety, failed; and Edmund Wilson acutely observes that in the stories he began to write immediately afterwards, sex and passion do make their appearance, often in a fashion that has (as in *The Turn of the Screw*) a faintly morbid flavour about it, but always at one remove: 'There are plenty of love affairs now and plenty of irregular relations, but there are always barriers between them and us; they are the chief object of interest, but they are seen from a distance.' This is exactly the case with *The Aspern Papers*, where the love affair between Jeffery Aspern and Juliana Bordereau, which is not only mysterious but placed at least two generations back in a glamorous past, is the focus of interest. To create this effect of passion *at a great distance* James uses all his extraordinary skill: the touch that has always impressed me most is the veiling of Juliana's eyes—the eyes which the poet had praised as so magnificent—until the terrible moment when she discovers the narrator trying to open the secretaire where the papers may be hidden, and they blaze forth 'like a sudden drench, for a caught burglar, of a flow of gaslight'. And even about Miss Bordereau, whose affair with Aspern was at any rate part of literary history and the inspiration of some of his most beautiful lyrics, there lingers an atmosphere not entirely in keeping with this sublimity, a suggestion of lawless or morbid passion the memory of which has had to be suppressed—may indeed be the secret of the closely guarded papers. The readers of Aspern's poetry have always felt that 'there hovered about her name a perfume of impenitent passion, an intimation that she had not been exactly as the respectable young person in general', and Miss Tina, her niece, admits, when questioned by the narrator as to the cause of Juliana's suspiciousness, that it has not been caused by indiscreet curiosity or persecution, but 'on account of something—ages ago, before I was born—in her life'.

It would be unwise to press what can only be, after all, a supposition, too far; but if I am right in thinking that *The Aspern Papers* reveals a breaking into two of James's own personality in the mirror of his art, and if Edmund Wilson is right in suggesting that just at the time when he wrote it James was allowing his artistic intuition or subconscious to present his own predicament of emotional failure in the pattern of his plots, then *The Aspern Papers* is the most intimate of all the stories, which include *The Turn of the*

Screw and *What Maisie Knew*, which James wrote under this compulsion, and the one which most fully reveals to us the tension between fantasy and reality, between an emotional trauma in the past (which may as much be James's own childhood as Aspern's Byronic age), and a neurosis of frustration in the present. This does not, of course, detract from the artistic brilliance of the story; on the contrary a constant re-reading of *The Aspern Papers* impresses me more and more with a quality which the greatest artists have always been able to give their work, of suggesting a number of different meanings at different levels simultaneously. The decayed Palazzo in Venice, overlooking the 'clean, melancholy rather lonely canal', seems to hold for one now not only a transposition of the Shelley legend but also a parable of James's emotional life, and beyond that again, perhaps, a parable of the mysterious workings of inspiration in the creative mind: Juliana says quite simply of Aspern that 'he was a god', and both her references to him and the narrator's worship invest him with a more than human effulgence, while the ghastly dénouement at the secretary has even a faint suggestion of the fatal discovery of Cupid in the legend of Cupid and Psyche.

Most of all, however, I find in *The Aspern Papers* a symbolic presentation of the glamour and decay of Europe's culture more richly and interestingly worked out than anywhere else in the work of an author who was peculiarly susceptible to such impressions. *The Aspern Papers* is a poem about Venice, in which Venice is chosen to represent supremely a quality which Henry James's imagination responds to in all the ancient cities of Europe; and it is just this achievement of creating a poem while writing a story which I judge to be so fine, and recognize as the second element of the two that have made me cherish *The Aspern Papers* so long above all James's other *novellen*. James is at the utmost pains to create the atmosphere of Venice, but it is done by a multitude of light touches and exquisitely judged brief descriptive passages, which never leave one with the slightly unpleasant feeling of having eaten too many sweets which the self-consciously 'atmospheric' writer is apt to produce. How naturally, and yet how unforgettably, Miss Bordereau's palazzo is introduced as Mrs. Prest and her friend first see it: 'The gondola stopped, the old palace was there; it was a house of the class which in Venice carries even in extreme dilapidation the dignified name. "How charming. How gray and pink!" my companion exclaimed; and that is the most comprehensive description of it. It was not particularly old, only two or three centuries; and it had an air not so much of decay as of quiet discouragement, as if it had rather missed its career. But its wide front, with a stone balcony from end to end of the *piano nobile* or most important floor, was architectural enough, with the aid of various pilasters and arches; and the stucco with which in the intervals it had long ago been endued was rosy in the April afternoon. . . .' And how full of poetry is such a passage as this: 'The great basilica, with its low domes and bristling embroideries, the mystery of its mosaic and sculpture, looked ghostly in the tempered gloom, and the sea-breeze passed between the twin columns of the Piazetta, the lintels of a door no longer guarded, as gently as if a rich curtain swayed there. . . .' Or, on the evening of the dénouement, how evocative in detailed observation the scene: 'We strolled through the fine superfluous hall, where on the marble floor—particularly as at first we said nothing—our footsteps were more audible than I had expected. When we reached the other end—the wide window, inevitably closed, connecting with the balcony that overhung the canal—I submitted that we had best remain there, as she would see the doctor arrive sooner. I opened the window and we passed out on the balcony. The air of the canal seemed even heavier, hotter than that of the sala. The place was hushed and void; the quiet neighbourhood had gone to sleep. A lamp, here and there, over the narrow black water, glimmered in double; the voice of a man going homeward singing, his jacket on his shoulder and his hat on his ear, came to us from a distance. . . .' And what could be more masterly than the final impression, as if in a summing up and to hint more strongly than ever at the foreground importance of the background theme, than these descriptive touches a few pages before the end: 'I don't know why it happened that on this occasion I was more than ever struck with that queer air of sociability, of cousinship and family life, which makes up half the expression of Venice. Without streets and vehicles, the uproar of wheels, the brutality of horses, and with its little winding ways where people crowd together, where voices sound as in the corridor of a house, where the human step circulates as if it skirted the angles of furniture and shoes never wear out, the place has the character of an immense collective apartment, in which Piazza San Marco is the most ornamented corner and palaces and churches, for the rest, play the part of great divans of repose, tables of entertainment, expanses of decoration. And somehow the expensive common domicile, familiar, domestic and resonant, also resembles a theatre with its actors clicking over bridges and, in straggling processions, tripping along fondamentas. As you sit in your gondola the footways that in certain parts edge the canals assume to the eye the importance of a stage, meeting it at the same angle, and the Venetian figures, moving to and fro against the battered scenery of their little houses of comedy, strike you as members of an endless dramatic troupe.'

It is difficult not to believe that this intention too, of creating a poem about Venice, was conscious in James's mind. 'The air', he says in his Preface, 'of the old-time Italy invests it, a mixture that on the faintest invitation I rejoice again to inhale—and this in spite of the mere cold renewal, ever, of the infirm side of that felicity, the sense, in the whole element, of things too numerous, too deep, too obscure, too strange, or even simply too beautiful, for any ease of intellectual relation.' How all the interwoven themes concur with that description of things 'too deep, too obscure, too strange, or even simply too beautiful', and call up the shimmering harmonies of Guardi's landscapes or the melancholy echoes of a sonnet by August von Platen. The miracle is that James is never precious, never—as so many latter day purveyors of poetic prose—indulgent to himself in elaborated beauties that distort the proportions of the story simply as a story; imagine it without the plot and you find at once how much the poetry loses —because the characters both in themselves and in their interaction are as 'pure' as any other element in the poetic whole. Juliana Bordereau herself is like the incarnation of Venice, of that Europe that held Henry James so ineluctably in its spell, and even her savage grasping after her American visitor's money, which brings her, by a masterly stroke of surprise, so vividly to life in their first interview, is in keeping; it is indeed at this point that the experiment of making her an American seems to break down, and one recalls the rather awkward apology James puts forward when he first introduces Miss Bordereau and her nieces: 'they were believed to have lost in their long exile all national quality, besides being as their name implied of some remote French affiliation.'

Henry James covered a great many tracks when he composed *The Aspern Papers*; but the important thing—as in all poetry—is not the definition but the suggestion of many meanings implied in one; and in creating such a prose poem James seems to me to have achieved what so many writers have groped after so ineffectually since his day, the solution of an artistic problem peculiar to our own age where the frontiers of poetry's territory are being driven steadily back till they appear to have shrunk to the compass of a Vatican City in relation to a whole secular state of Italy, the state of prose: the translation into terms of prose and plot of a poetic apprehension. *The Aspern Papers* is a new invention, a sonnet of the novel.

On Re-Reading 'The Rover'

Why does one suddenly begin re-reading an author one has left on the shelves for a whole decade or more? Sometimes, it seems, after an early and absorbing enthusiasm, one is so saturated with an author's works that they exist more in one's mind than in the printed volumes; and if one starts to re-read, the pages seem dry and lifeless beside the peopled landscape they have formed in one's memory. One drops them at last; one turns to other authors and the dust accumulates over them; but all the time, as the inner landscape grows imperceptibly more remote, more blurred, curiosity and the stirring of a taste once stimulated so strongly, begin to increase without one's knowing it. It is like the pressure in a closed saucepan as it is brought slowly to the boil: suddenly the lid can withstand the steam no longer, and out the water foams with a clatter and hiss.

Something like that, at any rate, happened to me with the works of Joseph Conrad. In my twenties I read him persistently, ardently. Gradually my enthusiasm tailed off, was crowded out by other enthusiasms; then at the beginning of the war I turned back to him, and found in *The End of the Tether*, *Victory*, *Lord Jim* and many of the shorter stories those qualities which make Conrad of such incomparable value at a time like that: his belief in courage, in loyalty, in the sea and the peoples who live by means of the sea. Night after night I went through the row of volumes in those months of menacing calm—in many ways so like the atmosphere Conrad loved to build up—more critical, perhaps, than I had been before of certain blemishes of overwriting, of those over-studied, over-painted effects that just betray the brilliant foreigner, but relishing far more and seeing further into the moral pattern that is behind all he wrote. Then, after 1940, I dropped him almost as suddenly as I had picked him up again; and it was not till the other day that—the saucepan suddenly boiling—I took *The Rover* down and began to read it.

My first reaction was, I think, surprise that I had denied myself such a pleasure for so long: a pleasure produced not only by the matter of the story but by Conrad's manner of unfolding it. But it was not long before I began to be aware of some other impression, an evocation that excited me though I could not at once place it. In his painting of Peyrol Conrad creates a background of indefinable romance and mystery by the touches, scattered all through the book, of his past as a Brother of the Coast. I doubt if he expected his readers to know what that name implied; perhaps he preferred them not to know, for he lets just enough information slip through for one to be able to form a picture of a lawless pirate life in the Indian Ocean, of comradeships in exotic dangers and a gathering together of strange adventurous lives outside the reach and restraint of civilized society. When Lieutenant Réal asks Peyrol whether he has ever been in prison:

> It roused Peyrol nearly into a shout. 'Heavens! No: Prison! What do you mean by prison. . . . I have been a captive to savages,' he added, calming down, 'but that's a very old story. I was young and foolish then. Later, when a grown man, I was a slave to the famous Ali-Kassim. I spent a fortnight in chains on my legs and arms in the yard of a mud fort on the shores of the Persian Gulf. There was nearly a score of us Brothers of the Coast in the same predicament. . . . There was not a single one of his thousand blackamoors that could lay a gun properly. But Ali-Kassim made war like a prince. We sailed, a regular fleet, across the gulf, took a town on the coast of Arabia somewhere, and looted it. Then I and the others managed to get hold of an armed dhow, and we fought our way right through the blackamoor's fleet. Several of us died of thirst later. All the same, it was a great affair. But don't you talk to me of prisons. A proper man if given a chance to fight can always get himself killed. . . .'

No more is added to this barbaric glimpse of Peyrol's youth; and then, a few chapters later, Peyrol's recognition of the English sailor who has been trapped in his tartane as a former brother gives Conrad the opportunity to add a few more illuminating touches, and to underline his characteristically Conradian conception of the

Brotherhood as an association of brave men above the pettiness of national hatreds:

The first suspicion of that amazing fact had intruded on Peyrol while he was bandaging that head by the light of the smoky lamp. Since the fellow still lived, it was not in Peyrol to finish him off or let him lie unattended like a dog. And then this was a sailor. His being English was no obstacle to the development of Peyrol's mixed feelings in which hatred certainly had no place. Amongst the members of the Brotherhood it was the Englishmen whom he preferred. He had also found amongst them that particular and loyal appreciation, which a Frenchman of character and ability will receive from Englishmen sooner than from any other nation. . . . And so that youngster had turned into this English man-of-war's man! In the fact itself there was nothing impossible. You found Brothers of the Coast in all sorts of ships and in all sorts of places. Peyrol had found one once in a very ancient and hopeless cripple practising the profession of a beggar on the steps of Manila cathedral; and had left him the richer by two broad gold pieces to add to his secret hoard. There was a tale of a Brother of the Coast having become a mandarin in China, and Peyrol believed it. One never knew where and in what position one would find a Brother of the Coast. . . .

A few pages later, there is another glimpse, skilfully introduced, which shows how thoroughly Conrad entered imaginatively into his characters, so that a passing simile naturally evokes a detail from memory:

The face of the farmhouse might have been the face of a house from which all the inhabitants had fled suddenly. In the high part of the building the window of the lieutenant's room remained open, both glass and shutter. By the door of the salle the stable fork leaning against the wall seemed to have been forgotten by the sans-culotte. This aspect of abandonment struck Peyrol with more force than usual. He had been thinking so hard of all these people that to find no one about seemed unnatural and even depressing. He had seen many abandoned places in his life, grass huts, mud forts, king's palaces—temples from which every white-robed soul had fled. Temples, however, never looked quite empty. The gods clung to their own. Peyrol's eyes rested on the bench against the wall of the salle. . . .

There are not more than three or four other such touches in the book, but their cumulative effect is powerful, giving Peyrol a legendary perspective in the mind of the reader, and continually throwing into relief the brooding stillness of the actual time of the narrative and the quality of charged interim about the half-dozen characters whose drama is acted out, with a slow fatality, against the almost empty scene. It is the way of poetry, a touching of chords that awaken echoes in the deeper chambers of the imagination, so that Peyrol himself assumes a symbolic character in a setting where, enveloped in Conrad's atmospheric prose, the farmstead 'like a lighthouse' at the end of the peninsula and the limitless horizons of sea also acquire the resonance of poetic symbols:

What made for him the life of any strange shore were the craft that belonged to it: canoes, catamarans, ballahous, praus, lorchas, mere dug-outs, or even rafts of tied logs with a bit of mat for a sail from which naked brown men fished along stretches of white sand crushed under the tropical skyline, sinister in its glare and with a thunder-cloud crouching on the horizon. But here he beheld a perfect serenity, nothing sombre on the shore, nothing ominous in the sunshine. The sky rested lightly on the distant and vaporous outline of the hills; and the immobility of all things seemed poised in the air like a gay mirage. On this tideless sea several tartanes lay becalmed in the Petite Passe between Porquerolles and Cape Esterel, yet there was not the stillness of death but of light slumber, the immobility of a smiling enchantment, of a Mediterranean fair day, breathless sometimes but never without life. Whatever enchantment Peyrol had known in his wanderings it had never been so remote from all thoughts of strife and death, so full of smiling security, making all his past appear to him like a chain of lurid days and sultry nights. He thought he would never want to get away from it. . . .

This 'smiling enchantment', with its unmistakeable reminiscences of Shelley's *Invitation*, is no less feelingly created, no less symbolically appropriate than its eventual reversal. Towards the climax of the book, as the drama quickens, Peyrol hears the thunderstorm that menaces his plans gathering in the west:

For a moment all his faculties seemed paralyzed by that faint sound. On that sea ruled by the gods of Olympus he might have been a pagan mariner subject to Jupiter's caprices; but like the defiant pagan he shook his fist vaguely at space which answered him by a short and threatening mutter. . . .

It was this passage which crystallized the thought that had been growing in my mind from the moment I had become aware of

Conrad's poetic approach to his theme, and gave me the answer to the problem that had been teasing me increasingly as I read through the book. The evocation, the parallel that excited me was, of course, to Homer. Was it not Odysseus returning at last to Ithaca, with all his fabulous doings in the Trojan War and his fabulous adventures on the homeward journey that Conrad's drawing of Peyrol suggested? And did not the conception of the brotherhood of gallant warriors call to mind some of the most famous encounters in the Iliad? In the great encounter between Diomedes and Glaucus, Glaucus entrances his Achaean adversary by the story of his legendary ancestor Bellerophon's exploits, and instead of fighting, discovering that their grandfathers had been friends, they leap down from their chariots and exchange armour. The discovery by Peyrol that Symons, the English sailor who has fallen into his hands, was also once a Brother, evokes exactly the same spirit: 'As against a wearer of epaulettes mutual protection was the first duty between Brothers of the Coast. The unexpectedness of that claim coming to him after twenty years invested it with an extraordinary strength.' Again, in the great set-piece at the end of *The Rover*, Conrad introduces the following dialogue between the captain of the corvette that has captured Peyrol's tartane and Nelson, present as admiral of the English blockading fleet:

'You have a very smart little ship, Vincent. Very fit for the work I have given you to do. French built, isn't she?'
'Yes, my lord. They are great shipbuilders.'
'You don't seem to hate the French, Vincent,' said the Admiral, smiling faintly.
'Not that kind, my lord,' said Captain Vincent with a bow. 'I detest their political principles and the characters of their public men, but your lordship will admit that for courage and determination we could not have found worthier adversaries anywhere on this globe.'
'I never said they were to be despised,' said Lord Nelson. 'Resource, courage, yes. . . .'

There is surely, behind this scene, exactly the same idea of an affinity behind all noble enmities that inspired the encounter in Book Seven of the *Iliad* between Hector and Ajax:

'Ajax,' said the great Hector of the flashing helmet, 'you are big, strong and able, and the best spearman on your side. Admitting that,

I suggest we cease fighting for the day, for we can always meet again and go on till the powers above decide between us. Also, the light is failing. We should do well to take the hint. The Achaeans would be very glad to see you back at the ships, your own friends and followers above all; while I should get a warm welcome in King Priam's city from the Trojans and the Trojan ladies in their trailing gowns, assembled for thanksgiving to the gods on my behalf. But first let us exchange gifts of honour, so that it may be said by Trojans and Achaeans alike that we two fought each other tooth and nail, but presently were reconciled and parted friends. . . .'

But if Peyrol, the hero of *The Rover*, has been given a legendary background of exotic violence, Conrad has matched him, not merely against the national English enemy, but against an adversary of far deeper and more fundamental opposition, the embittered ex-sansculotte Scevola. He, too, is given by his creator a background of only half-suggested violence, but of a very different sort. Scevola is painted as a doctrinaire agent of the Terror, obsessed by the simplified intellectual patterns of the Revolution, a fanatic who believes that at the bottom of every trouble can be found an 'aristo' and to whom the only 'patriots' are the sansculottes like himself who were prepared to murder an 'aristo' on sight, without trial or question. Everything is confused into conspiracy against the Revolution in his one-track mind: working himself up into a frenzy because he suspects that Lieutenant Réal has a secret liaison with Arlette, he paces up and down outside the farmhouse in the night:

He became giddy with virtuous fury. There was enough evidence there for any revolutionary tribunal to cut all their heads off. Tribunal! There was no Tribunal! No revolutionary justice! No patriots! He hit his shoulder against the wall in his distress with such force that he rebounded. This world was no place for patriots. . . .

The irony of Scevola's position is that what he stands for is already old-fashioned. The bright ideals and bloodstained savageries of the Revolution are receding into the past as Bonaparte's star steadily rises. He sees the priests restored to their churches, the witch-hunts against the 'aristos' called off, and people openly daring to ignore and despise the untainted servants of revolutionary passion such as himself—even muttering against him for his former butcheries. It is from Arlette, the child whose parents he had been instrumental in doing to death during the Toulon terror, and whom he had afterwards married, that we get our brief, lurid glimpses of the horrors of those days and nights that already seem as legendary as Peyrol's exploits in the Brotherhood of the Coast. For Arlette they have been a nightmare so terrible that they have frozen the deepest springs in her nature; it is only when she is conscious of her love for the lieutenant that she tries to withdraw this obstruction by telling her story to the Abbé:

'The bodies of her father and mother were lying across the doorway. The room was full of gunpowder smoke. She wanted to fling herself on the bodies and cling to them, but Scevola took her under the arm and lifted her over them. He seized her hand and made her run with him, or rather dragged her downstairs. Outside on the pavement some dreadful men and many fierce women with knives joined them. They ran along the streets brandishing pikes and sabres, pursuing other groups of unarmed people, who fled round corners with loud shrieks:

'I ran in the midst of them, Monsieur l'Abbé,' Arlette went on in a breathless murmur. 'Whenever I saw any water I wanted to throw myself into it, but I was surrounded on all sides, I was jostled and pushed and most of the time Scevola held my hand very tight. When they stopped at a wine shop, they would offer me some wine. My tongue stuck to the roof of my mouth and I drank. The wine, the pavements, the arms and the faces, everything was red. I had red splashes all over me. I had to run with them all day, and all the time I felt as if I were falling down, and down, and down. The houses were nodding at me. The sun would go out at times. And suddenly I heard myself yelling exactly like the others. Do you understand, Monsieur l'Abbé? The very same words!'

In *The Rover* Conrad might, at first sight, be thought only to be telling one of his masterly atmospheric stories of seafaring, conspiracy and romance; but the deeper moral pattern is, it seems to me, worked out with great care though never obtrusively. After her traumatic experiences in Toulon as a child, Arlette is brought back to life by her love for Réal, and that love absolves her guilt of blood. Parallel with her redemption is Peyrol's: he is brought back from his aimless, retired existence on the farmstead into action and new identification with his beloved France by the plot to deceive the English fleet; and his death in that action, inspired both by patriotic devotion and selfless love for Arlette, absolves the lawless, pirate exploits of his youth.

Equally important—perhaps all-important—is the contrast between Peyrol and Scevola; and one cannot escape the impression that by pitting these two men against one another, Conrad was dramatizing a conflict about which he had brooded a great deal and which he had come to believe went down to the roots of life. It is an essentially modern theme, more vivid and urgent to us now, perhaps, even than when Conrad wrote, the subject of some of the greater novels of our time, such as *The Power and the Glory*: the opposition of the man of heart and the man of head in a revolutionary time. Scevola is a bigot of the idea: he has committed murders without number in the name of Liberty, Equality and Fraternity, and is prepared, years later, to commit more in order that the Revolution shall not be corrupted by the slow insidious action of life and time. No matter to him if the cruelties and injustices he demands are worse even than those the Revolution originally came about to eradicate: he is one who is entirely absorbed in the idea of the best, and has never heard of the saying that the best is the worst enemy of the good. Peyrol has also committed crimes enough in his equally fabulous past: he has slaughtered, he has destroyed, he has robbed, but the difference is defined by Réal as he meditates on the way a web of sympathies and more highly charged emotions is gradually entangling him at the farmhouse: 'He had developed a liking for old Peyrol, the only man who had nothing to do with the revolution—who had not even seen it at work. The sincere lawlessness of the ex-Brother of the Coast was refreshing. That one was neither a hypocrite nor a fool. When he robbed or killed it was not in the name of the sacred revolutionary principles or for the love of humanity.' It would have been easy enough to contrast Scevola with a man whose hands were unstained with blood. Conrad went one further: he wanted to extract a deeper condemnation of Scevola's sort. The final kidnapping of Scevola on to the tartane, as it goes out on the mission from which Peyrol knows it cannot return, is a convenient device to prepare the way for the happily-ever-after ending for Arlette and Réal; but it also gives an extra ironical twist to Scevola's story and puts in a final brilliant spotlight the fundamental contrast between the two men. This end has the justice and power of a great poetic tragedy. It is profoundly symbolical; and if Captain Vincent and Admiral Lord Nelson utter the last words on the Homeric theme of honourable enmity—a sentiment that could never have had any echo in Scevola's heart, any more than in the hearts of the ideological fanatics of newer Tribunals who have succeeded him today—Conrad himself, in the last paragraph of the book, like the last brief chorus of a Greek play, has the last word on his hero, Peyrol:

> The blue level of the Mediterranean, the charmer and the deceiver of audacious men, kept the secret of its fascination—hugged to its calm breast the victims of all the wars, calamities and tempests of its history, under the marvellous purity of the sunset sky. A few rosy clouds floated high up over the Esterel range. The breath of the evening breeze came to cool the heated rocks of Escampobar, and the mulberry tree, the only big tree on the head of the peninsula, standing like a sentinel at the gate of the yard, sighed faintly in a shudder of all its leaves, as if regretting the Brother of the Coast, the man of dark deeds, but of large heart, who often at noonday would lie down to sleep under its shade.

The Most Austere School

'The idea of a popular art,' wrote Proust in the last volume of his huge work, 'like that of a patriotic art, even if it were not dangerous, seems to me absurd.'

When I first came across those words, they gave me that shock of pure delight one receives when a friend suddenly, by an unexpected remark, reveals that all along he has been burrowing into the same problems as oneself, and has come to the same conclusion—but puts them more boldly and categorically than one has dared to as yet in one's own still misty formulations. It was the middle of the last war, the first time I had read *Time Regained*, though by no means the beginning of my acquaintance with *Remembrance of Things Past*; I perceived the irony of the fact that if I had read right through to the last volume when I first embarked on Proust's work, so many years before, the shock would have been rather of outrage and refusal to believe, unless indeed the point and wit of the argument had broken past the internal censor and saved one from the fruitless chasing after many false scents. I had, however, picked up the volumes erratically, at long intervals, between other reading and other pursuits; and thus it happened that I came to Proust's immense investigation of the nature of art and the task of the artist at the perfect psychological moment, when the truths he proclaimed seemed most necessary, the authority he gave them as powerful as one could wish.

It was a time when our Russian allies, as they then were, could lend the effulgence of their military prestige to their views on many other aspects of doing and thinking. The irrelevance was not always immediately apparent. And their views on literature and art were most emphatically in favour of their being both popular and patriotic. Their official retorts to those who raised any doubts about this, as I later had good reason to discover from my own lamentable experience, were vitriolic; and yet I have wondered whether, among the writers then living, and still living within the confines of the Soviet despotism, there were not one or two left, survivals from a freer age, who could remember with a smile that Proust, so far from thinking that 'popular' art was what the masses needed or wanted, maintained that its true appeal (granted, of course, the right subject material) was to the rich and shallow social world, had in fact written that 'a popular art form should rather be intended for members of the Jockey Club than for those of the General Confederation of Labour'.

In England luckily, in spite of the glories of Stalingrad, common sense, a sturdy sceptical tradition—and a sense of humour—prevented such doctrines gaining much headway at the time. Nevertheless, their considerable success in many countries of Europe, and the continuance, in fact aggravation of conditions in the world generally that demand a playing down to popular sentiment and at the same time a strengthening by all possible means of national, patriotic solidarity, make Proust's definitions of supreme importance for our age.

Marcel Proust, it will be remembered, only conceived the plan, amassed the notes and started the writing of *Remembrance of Things Past* when he was in his middle thirties. He had been written off by the literary world—or so he fancied—as a rich dilettante, author of some pieces of exquisite prose, who would never get down to a proper job of work. Then, just as he was beginning to despair, the double revelation, it seems, came to him: that the book he was to write had been ripening all the time within the deepest layers of his mind, out of the significant memories and apprehensions of beauty of his childhood and youth; and that Time was to be the framework into which these intuitions of reality were to be fitted, Time the element in which everything was to be steeped.

This discovery, and the preparation for the work which was to take him the remainder of his life and to involve a change in his way of living as complete, a regimen as rigorous as the entry into a monastery, is the subject of *Time Regained*. Though some of the details may have been changed, to comply with the minimum demands of the fictional form of art which he had chosen, we can assume that what the narrator sets forth was substantially Proust's own experience. The size and complexity of the undertaking to which he, a frail invalid, was determined to dedicate the rest of his years and powers, overwhelmed him while it excited him:

> Finally this idea of Time had the ultimate value of the hand of a clock. It told me it was time to begin if I meant to attain that which I had felt in brief flashes on the Guermantes' side and during my drives with Mme de Villeparisis, that indefinable something which had made me think life worth living. How much more so now that it seemed possible to illuminate that life lived in darkness, at last to make manifest in a book the truth that one ceaselessly falsifies. Happy the man who could write such a book. What labour awaited him. To convey its scope would necessitate comparison with the noblest and most various arts. For the writer, in creating each character, would have to present it from conflicting standpoints so that his book should have solidity, he would have to prepare it with meticulous care, perpetually regrouping his forces as for an offensive, to bear it as a load, to accept it as the object of his life, to build it like a church, to follow it like a regime, to overcome it like an obstacle, to win it like a friendship, to nourish it like a child, to create it like a world, mindful of those mysteries which probably only have their explanation in other worlds, the presentiment of which moves us most in life and in art. Parts of such great books can be no more than sketched for time presses and perhaps they can never be finished because of the very magnitude of the architect's design. . . . The very thought of my edifice never left me for an instant. I did not know whether it would be a church where the faithful would gradually learn truth and discover the harmony of a great unified plan or whether it would remain, like a Druid monument on the heights of a desert island, unknown for ever. But I had made up my mind to consecrate to it the power that was ebbing away, reluctantly almost, as though to leave me time to elaborate the structure before the entrance to the tomb was sealed. I was soon able to show an outline of my project. No one understood it. . . .

From that moment of dedication, Marcel Proust became one of the great heroes of the life of art, whose famous victories—did he not envisage himself as a general 'perpetually regrouping his forces'?—can now be seen as Time, his own chosen ally, uncovers the magnitude of his achievement, to loom as large in the history of the modern mind as those of any Foch or Eisenhower in the field. And in completing that offensive, as part of the final encircling movement, he elaborated his view of the sacred task of the creative writer, trapping in his 'pocket' the disordered regiments of journalism, politics, society with their associated detachments of every sort and kind of pseudo-art. I do not know of any exposition in our time of this fundamental creed as subtle, eloquent, comprehensive and witty. Poor M. de Norpois, with his simple theories 'against flute-players': there is not much left of the vain old diplomatist's worldly views when Proust has done with him. Poor Bloch, with his contempt for the portrayal of 'insignificant idlers' in literature: his remark: 'I avow that the portraits of these futile people are indifferent to me'—becomes in Proust's hands a classic fatuity. The preachers of 'engagement' who denounce the 'ivory tower', the superior philistines who see in the greatest art only a pernicious form of 'escapism', the muddled and angry social idealists who clamour for novels about 'great working-class movements', the theorist critics who cannot value a poem or a novel unless it contains an overt intellectual message or philosophy are all disarmed, routed and eliminated. They require the meaning of a work, says Proust quietly, 'to be expressed in direct terms because they are unable to infer it from the beauty of imagery. Hence that vulgar temptation of an author to write intellectual works. A great indelicacy.'

Proust's view of art and reality, though strongly influenced, it has often been said, by the philosophies of Darlu and Bergson, was no startling revaluation. He only asserted, and put into contemporary terms, a belief that had been held by many great artists in previous generations. His debt to Ruskin was profound and openly acknowledged. Demetrios Capetanakis, in his brilliant *Lecture on Proust*, has pointed out how close his basic conceptions are to 'those of the Wordsworth who wrote the *Ode on the Intimations of Immortality*'. He is anticipated again by Shelley, so much of whose *Defence of Poetry* is an attempt to elucidate the same theme. It was Shelley, also, who wrote, in *Prometheus Unbound*, of the poet:

> He will watch from dawn to gloom
> The lake-reflected sun illume
> The yellow bees in the ivy bloom,
> Nor heed, nor see, what things they be;
> But from these create he can
> Forms more real than living man,
> Nurslings of immortality.

It is precisely when he describes how, even in his early days at Combray, he was trying to discover under images that haunted him 'a thought which these objects were expressing in the manner of hieroglyphic characters', that he comes to his key passage:

> That book of unknown signs within me (signs in relief it seemed, for my concentrated attention, as it explored my unconscious in its search, struck against them, circled round them like a diver sounding) no one could help me to read by any rule, for its reading consists in an act of creation in which no one can take our place and in which no one can collaborate. And how many turn away from writing it, how many tasks will one not assume to avoid that one! Every event, whether it was the Dreyfus affair or the war, furnished excuses for writers for not deciphering that book; they wanted to assert the triumph of Justice, to recreate the moral unity of the nation and they had no time to think of literature. But those were only excuses because either they did not possess or had ceased to possess genius, that is, instinct. For it is instinct which dictates duty and intelligence which offers pretexts for avoiding it. But excuses do not exist in art, intentions do not count there, the artist must at all times follow his instinct, which makes art the most real thing, the most austere school in life and the true last judgement. That book which is the most arduous of all to decipher is the only one which reality has dictated, the only one printed within us by reality itself. . . .

It has been said that genius will out, like murder; but it seems much more likely that genius, like any other plant, needs the most assiduous tending and can be spoilt by too little watering, too little sunshine, cold east winds and a badly prepared soil. Good soil conditions—and the ancient civilization of Europe must provide a humus as rich as any that has ever existed—can deteriorate rapidly if mismanaged; it is in fact difficult to imagine a speedier deterioration in conditions than has taken place in Europe during the last few generations. If there were black storms and cold winds blowing in the time of Proust's youth, they have blown with greater violence during the youth of the present generation. The Dreyfus affairs have grown into Spanish and Korean wars, the need to 'assert the triumph of Justice' has become ever more difficult to resist, the siren-call of journalism, magnified enormously by the development of broadcasting, with all the immediate publicity and importance that attaches to the name at the head of the feature article, the radio voice that reveals the inside story, that loud and raucous tune has been too much for all but the most inflexible-willed Odysseus lashed with the tightest of cords to his mast. It may reasonably be objected that it is for the good of humanity that Justice should be vindicated, oppression denounced and the truth declared by the sharpest eye and quickest intelligence; all these objections are true, but for the artist the paramount truth is that the best way for him to serve humanity is to serve his art, to be true to 'that book of unknown signs' within him and to stop his ears to the never-ending clamour about 'escapism' and 'ivory towers'. It was Shelley again, of all people, who said that 'the exertions of Locke, Hume, Gibbon, Voltaire, Rousseau, and their disciples, in favour of oppressed and deluded humanity, are entitled to the gratitude of mankind. . . . But it exceeds all imagination to conceive what would have been the moral condition of mankind if neither Dante, Petrarch, Boccaccio, Chaucer, Shakespeare, Calderon, Lord Bacon, nor Milton, had ever existed.'

What is wrong with our age is not that here and there an ivory tower still, astonishingly, survives, but that far too many have been reduced to rubble; for, as Proust said, 'real books must be children not of broad daylight and small-talk but of darkness and silence'.

There is, however, it seems to me, another and more difficult objection to be faced. It is clear that Proust's views were designed to fit Proust's own case as closely as possible; and the book that Proust discovered he had to write was a vast recreation of his own life, an autobiography—admittedly of interior realities and not outward appearances—only slightly reshaped into the form of fiction. It may be true that Bergotte is Renan and perhaps even Proust himself as well as Anatole France, and that Monsieur de Charlus is Robert de Montesquiou and Baron Doazan, and has characteristics and meets experiences that were taken from other now forgotten denizens of the Cities of the Plain; the chief characters may be composite pictures and Proust may have divided his own characteristics up among several of them; but basically the story remains autobiography, and Proust's admirable recipe for reading the 'book of unknown signs' would appear to produce only works in which the subject is the artist himself. This is all very well for the poet, but can it be adequate advice for the novelist, or dramatist, whose business it is to create a new imaginary world in each novel or play—unless, as Proust did, he stretches his own life story out from volume to volume? Since Proust died there have been, one may well argue, far too many novelists who never get beyond the book that tells the story of their own childhood and youth, and one can certainly attribute this in part to the prestige of his great work. His advice does not seem, at first sight, to be valid for a Shakespeare, a Dickens, a Flaubert, a Chekhov, a Henry James or a Virginia Woolf.

It is probably not possible to answer this objection completely. The processes of artistic creation are obscure and likely to remain so, in spite of such works of detective genius as Livingstone-Lowes's *The Road to Xanadu*, and the devoted but pedantic and uninspired explorations of many a research scholar on both sides of the Atlantic. Proust himself does not give us much help, as the works he refers to as admired exemplars—Chateaubriand's *Mémoires d'Outre-Tombe*, Baudelaire's poems and Ruskin's *Stones of Venice* and *Praeterita*—are none of them works of fiction, any more than Vermeer's paintings which he adored so much: they are all magical recreations of the artist's personal experience. And yet I believe that the objection is more imaginary than real. If the artist is true to his vision; that is, if his work is dictated by the restless searchings of his own mind and by the ceaseless flowerings of his own imagination, then the situation he creates, the symbols he introduces, rising irradiated from those deeper levels where all experience is unconsciously transformed, will have aesthetic truth and partake of those profound moral judgements and perceptions of beauty which are our most precious instinct and intuition. It is the refusal to work those seams because of the surface calls of the moment, the falsification of the judgement and perception for the sake of accepted codes and popular demands, and the permitting of political or social interest to dictate the shape and meaning of a work rather than instinct—these are the crimes and it is this criminal code that Proust insists on for the artist, and which is valid for the artist whether he is writing *Praeterita* or *Mrs. Dalloway*, *Mémoires d'Outre-Tombe* or *The Turn of the Screw*, *The Prelude* or *The Gentleman from San Francisco*.

And in making this stand, with such wit and wisdom, such uncompromising faith, Proust was achieving more than the justification of his own great work. He was giving lucid and courageous sailing instructions to a whole generation in danger of being driven right off their course by buffeting gales and tidal currents of unparalleled violence. In the face of the ambitious reporter with the popular knack, whose undigested sandwich packet of personal experiences, inchoate emotions and pretentious moral deductions are passed off as great literature; of the self-important critic in whom the lack of any true understanding of aesthetic values has turned into a bitterness, fanned by flattering politicians, against all genuine creators; of the poet caught in every gust of topical controversy, whose ear for the music of his unique inspiration has been deadened by the clamour of a hundred platforms; of the legion of clever novelists who can dress up the fashionable issues and attitudes of the day into fiction that scoops in all the prizes; in the face of the quacks, the counterfeiters, the just men confused and the men of power setting their springes, the voice of the night-haunting invalid in the cork-lined workroom, living on coffee and milk and Evian water, is heard quietly, almost maliciously observing that 'the work of our pride, our passion, our spirit of imitation, our abstract intelligence, our habits must be undone by art which takes the opposite course, and returning to the depths where the real has its unknown being, makes us pursue it'.

Portrait of the Artist as an Escaper

Over the mantelpiece in a room where I often work, there is a pencil drawing of James Joyce by Augustus John, one of a famous set. It is a very fine drawing indeed, and holds the eye by its flair and vitality, by the direct aesthetic satisfaction it gives. It is a balm to the mind when some problem with which one is wrestling refuses to yield, and one lifts one's gaze away from the scribbled papers in front of one to its bold and lucid statement.

And yet, below the surface satisfaction, it poses a problem as teasing as any that is ever likely to come the way of a critic, or anyone interested in the motives and ideals that underlie the life-pattern of men of genius. The high forehead, slightly furrowed as in argument or inquiry, the thin straight lips, the long and rather obstinate chin, suggest at once a vigorous and combative intellect, remind one indeed that Joyce's whole work is a triumph of intellectual energy and sustained will-power. Open the *Portrait of the Artist as a Young Man*, and it hits you in the eye at once; grapple with a few pages of *Finnegan's Wake*, and you can hardly fail to be convinced that the mind which created that extraordinary prose must be as uncommon as that of a Senior Wrangler. But how did the man who wrote the former come to write the latter? That is the mystery; how the lucidity, the passion, the quick feeling for character and dramatic effect that Joyce displayed so brilliantly at the outset of his career, flowered—perhaps seeded would be the juster word—into the vast obscurities, the fantastically perverse ingenuities that need almost a lifetime of patient study to elucidate and appreciate?

I can think of no case in the whole of literature that can be compared with Joyce's. Has any other writer so completely changed not only his style, but also the very words, the language he used? The later novels of Henry James show, indeed, a richly foliated evolution in style from the starting point of *Roderick Hudson* and *The American*. James grows subtler, more passionately tireless in pursuit of the slightest nuances of atmosphere, feeling, and moral distinction, and more long-winded in the bad sense of the word as well; but the author of *The Wings of the Dove* is recognizably the same author, he is still interested in creating the same kind of illusion of reality, and if his sentences have become so luxuriantly more qualified and complex, they only exaggerate a tendency that was always there; above all there is no refashioning of the basic tools of a writer's craft—no invention of the language itself. So with Mallarmé: though the art may become more arcane as the artist abandons himself to his morbid cravings—and by that I mean that he grows less and less interested in the necessities of communication—there are certain conventions he never rejects: the chief one being the French vocabulary into which he was born.

Shakespeare, perhaps, is the nearest parallel; for Shakespeare, living at a time when the English language was still in process of creation, or was recreating itself, was continually inventing words and phrases—how many it is difficult for us to tell, as his contemporaries have not left us any observations on the subject. In addition to this, towards the end of his working life his thought became deeper, more allusive and more daring in the leaps it took in the course of an argument, so that some of the speeches and soliloquies in *Cymbeline* or *A Winter's Tale* first of all dazzle us by their brilliance then leave us bewildered about their precise meaning. Shakespeare travelled a long way, in style, in thought, in language in the two decades between *Love's Labour's Lost* and Prospero's renunciation; and yet even this evolution—leaving aside all questions of relative aesthetic value—is not so rapid, so complex or so strange as the evolution of James Joyce.

The drawing by John does certainly give me a clue: for one of its most striking felicities is the way it suggests Joyce's *blindness*. It would, I think, be rash to claim that the gradual failure of sight, of visual appreciation of the external world, was entirely responsible for the evolution of Joyce's style; it is even just possible that both phenomena spring from one ulterior cause, hidden in the deeper recesses of the will and temperament; nevertheless it is undoubtedly true that Joyce as a writer grows more and more preoccupied with what goes on inside the mind, and that his genius, like an excavator digging ever further away from the daylight and the concrete daylight world, descends from one internal level of consciousness to another, even darker—to that level within sound of the subterranean streams which boil up only rarely but with incalculable force, as the psychologists tell us, to disrupt or fertilize the surface world. That is the progress of James Joyce from *Dubliners* and the *Portrait* through *Ulysses* to *Finnegan's Wake*, from Stephen Dedalus with his so clearly defined home background, hopes, fears and intellectual prejudices, to H. C. Earwicker, a phantasmal symbol of the universal subconscious in which all cultures and all languages merge and all passions swirl together without distinction or controlling order. *Finnegan's Wake* is the work of a man to whom night had become more important than day.

In a sense, of course, as critics have pointed out before now, it is all foretold in the *Portrait*; not only the self-imposed exile from Ireland, but the aesthetic conceptions that were to give birth to the two most uncomfortable masterpieces of our time. 'I will try to express myself', cries Stephen to his friend Cranly, 'in some mode of life or art as freely as I can and as wholly as I can, using for my defence the only arms I allow myself to use, silence, exile and cunning.' And in an earlier argument with his friends he says: 'When the soul of a man is born in this country there are nets flung at it to hold it back from the light. You talk to me of nationality, language, religion. I shall try to fly by those nets.'

And with the same passion and the steel-hard force of will with which he endowed Stephen, Joyce himself flew by the narrow-meshed net of his country's religion, his country's romantic national legend, and the language into which he had been born. What is important to notice about these ruthless and absolute renunciations is that they were not conversions: he did not put Protestantism in the place of Catholicism, he did not allow another country to adopt him, as so many intellectuals turning their backs on the jigsaw puzzle walls of Europe have allowed America to adopt them, he did not write in another language as Conrad learnt to write in English; his aim was to fly by all religions, all nationalities, all languages. *Ulysses* is his declaration of escape from the first two; and *Finnegan's Wake* from the last.

Independence from anything that may confine the free play of thought and imagination is vital to an artist; but in the peculiar and extravagant form in which Joyce pursued it with such violence of will, it had its terrible dangers. It is likely that he recognized them; it would be typical of his uncommon makeup to do so—and to defy them. I do not see what other interpretation can be put on the outburst with which Stephen concludes his argument with Cranly: 'I will tell you also what I do not fear. I do not fear to be alone or to be spurned for another or to leave whatever I have to leave. And I am not afraid to make a mistake, even a great mistake, a lifelong mistake and perhaps as long as eternity too.'

The bitter longings of Stephen Dedalus were the plans that James Joyce carried through to the end. He escaped from Ireland, and from Ireland's religion; but he never *freed* himself from them. He created works that were cosmopolitan in an entirely new sense; and yet the scene of the action in *Ulysses* is Dublin, and in *Finnegan's Wake* it is still Dublin, though more insubstantial and only fleetingly glimpsed. Dublin was the *omphalos* of his world to the end. No cosmopolitan writer has ever shown such an attachment to one place—and that one place his own home. And in his escape from Ireland's religion he did not take refuge in an all too civilized cynicism or a mystique of the aristocratic virtues, an internationalism of the cultivated mind. *The Portrait* reveals to us how deep was his need to put something in the place of the Catholic vision of the universe; he had been, one feels, so conditioned by the carefully constructed order of Jesuit teaching, that order, a different order but as exacting and elaborate as possible, was what he found he had to create for himself—not freedom. *Ulysses* is a monument of obsessive learning, of layer upon layer of symbolical parallels and allusive patterns, and his commentators have reverently pointed out to us the innumerable references to ancient religion and magic buried in it. Faust himself did not chalk out his mystic circles more passionately than did James Joyce in preparing a metaphysical scaffolding for his thinking once the Jesuit props had been torn away. And yet all this elaboration and erudition, the delight of the high priests of his memory, is almost totally irrelevant to the value of *Ulysses* as a work of art. What is true of *Ulysses* is true also of *Finnegan's Wake* in an even greater degree. Beside the great artist, another spirit, a mixture of Holofernes and Glendower, prepares his boringly ingenious examination papers and intones his abracadabras, and one begins to wish that Joyce had not been so ruthlessly determined to risk that mistake 'as long as eternity'.

Considered in cold blood, when one's excitement and amazement at the incredible virtuoso display have died away, *Ulysses* and *Finnegan's Wake*, which are certainly works of genius, are also staggering examples of misdirected genius—as Blake's Prophetic Books were. The pyramid of literature has grown huger since Blake's day, and the heirs of a civilization facing the possibility of absolute annihilation have become at the same time poorer in the leisure and concentration needed to climb that pyramid. How happy one might be, in the millenium, with no worries about food or money and no bureaucratic persecution, with all the advantages of science and none of its monstrous terrors, to devote seven years of tranquil study and appreciation to *Ulysses* and *Finnegan's Wake*. As it is, though many passages will remain in the anthologies, like Blake's Prophetic Books they are likely to be read in the future only by the specialist or research-endowed student, the lover of the recondite for the sake of the recondite, and those rare artists who are always searching for the stimulus to new technical achievement. There is nothing second-rate about the ambition behind these stupendous projects, nor about the intellect and the will that carried them through. It is indeed only when one has grasped the tremendous intellectual and artistic equipment of James Joyce, when one has understood how much of the literature of our day has some blood from *Ulysses* in its veins, when one has been bewitched by the author's own reading of the famous passages from *Finnegan's Wake* so luckily preserved for us on gramophone recordings, that one can properly appreciate the tragedy of the compulsions that led him to pour all those gifts into such forbidding and unwieldy bottles. The pedantry, the monotony, the mumbo-jumbo, the wanton surrender to the cross-word puzzle part of the mind—these also sprang from the 'silence, exile and cunning'. James Joyce did indeed escape from all the bars that seemed to be

Mary Mellish
Archibald
Memorial

imprisoning his youthful genius, but the attempt was as mad as Rimbaud's, and as in Rimbaud's case the natural order of things had its revenge and saw to it that the escaper himself built a new, perhaps a more terrible prison round his freedom.

Edward Thomas

I suppose I had met Edward Thomas in the anthologies, and admired the pieces anthologies always choose, such as *Out in the Dark* and *Lights Out*, some time before he began to speak to me with a voice that seemed to respond more and more subtly to my own feelings about *things*—old houses, hidden streams, woods under rain, bonfires in gardens and twisting country lanes—than that of any other poet I had read. I cannot now date the change and the revelation for myself; I only know there was a time when he was one among twenty or thirty Georgian poets I was reading with enthusiasm in the first flush of my discovery of what was then modern poetry, and that he is now one of the only three or four of those poets I still read and come back to again and again with delight and wonder.

There are nature poets in our literature who have made one particular landscape of England their own special raw material; the East Anglian coast found its poetic transmuter supremely in Crabbe, the Lakes in Wordsworth; the southern counties, the England of the Thames Valley, the Icknield Way and the Pilgrims' Way, the Cotswolds, the Chilterns and the South Downs, with their mildness of climate, their lush sweetness of nature, their gentle variety of contour, and their so unsensational antiquity of habitation and cultivation have been celebrated by more poets than one can count, but by none—so I have felt now for almost two decades—with more intimate and understanding love than by Edward Thomas. This, for me, a southerner by birth and upbringing with the Thames running in my veins, was a powerful argument of sympathy with Thomas's poetry; but there was not only the general compatibility, there was also the particular response, which I met with in no other poet. When I read the poem beginning:

> They have taken the gable from the roof of clay
> On the long swede pile. They have let in the sun
> To the white and gold and purple of curled fronds
> Unsunned. . . .

or the poem called *Digging*, which is still as exciting to me as when I first turned the page to it:

> To-day I think
> Only with scents,—scents dead leaves yield,
> And bracken, and wild carrot's seed,
> And the square mustard field;
>
> Odours that rise
> When the spade wounds the root of tree,
> Rose, currant, raspberry or goutweed,
> Rhubarb or celery. . . .

then I knew that at last I had found a fellow human being who had the same feeling that I had about the part of the garden beyond the lawn and the flower-border, and could, moreover, make exquisite poetry of it.

There was also something else about Thomas's nature poetry that drew me strongly towards it: an intensity of feeling, entirely different from the happy hiker's appreciation of green fields and birds twittering in the copses, something that suggested that he found in nature a spiritual revelation so important that the world might be meaningless if it were to disappear. And at the same time this intensity was expressed with the utmost simplicity and transparency, an absence of rhetorical flourishes and ingenious elaboration that enormously heightened the conviction it carried:

> I neither expected anything
> Nor yet remembered: but some goal
> I touched then; and if I could sing
> What would not even whisper my soul
> As I went on my journeying,
> I should use, as the trees and birds did,
> A language not to be betrayed;
> And what was hid should still be hid
> Excepting from those like me made
> Who answer when such whispers bid.

I did not at that time know how much the long friendship with Robert Frost, which began just before the 1914 war, helped Thomas to find himself in this style and perfect it; nor did I altogether realize the truth that, if the unemphatic, almost conversational tone was the most powerful method Thomas could have found to express his deepest feelings, such a tone would mean nothing at another level without the passionate intensity, would, in fact, be more tedious and unmemorable than conventional couplets and quatrains. But the discovery of such poems as *The Brook*, *October*, and *Over the Hill* set me in a distrust of the elaborately wrought and euphuistic manner which has found so many practitioners since Thomas's day (though I willingly admit the great beauty of some notable exceptions), and created a decisive ferment in my imagination at a time when I was looking for my own style in poetry and the solution of problems of approach that every generation has to face afresh—but seemed then peculiarly difficult to me.

The mastery which Thomas displayed in this kind of writing, the skill with which he chose words for their precise appropriateness without ever neglecting their overtones, the melody and harmonious texture of the whole, had been prepared by his long wearisome years of work to order and against the clock in prose. It is more usual in our time for a man who is going to make his mark as a prose writer to start by composing verse, and not the other way round; it is also commonly found that for a poet to have to apply himself persistently and without hope of relief to the turning out of journalism will ruin his ear and dry up the deeper springs of his imagination. The case of Edward Thomas contradicts all these propositions. He was in his late thirties before he began to write poetry; the remarkable absence of any fumbling at the start, even though his mastery increased in the two or three years that remained of his life, can be directly attributed to the experience in self-expression that his prose works—sometimes three, four and even five in a year—had given him; and a poet who could write *Two Houses*, *The Dark Forest* or *Roads* after such exhausting labours cannot be accused of having lost his ear or wasted his intuitive powers. It is an astonishing phenomenon, and proves that Thomas was a man of exceptional creative force; but one should also remember that most of the prose that he was obliged to write for a living was, except in such rare cases as his study of Swinburne where he seemed totally unmatched with his theme, on subjects that were naturally sympathetic to him: the countryside and the people who lived in it, and writers like Richard Jefferies who had loved the countryside as he did himself. There are even a number of extremely interesting parallels between the prose and the poetry, where the later poet-Thomas re-works in verse themes and moods which the essayist-Thomas had expressed in prose many years before: it is as if, in the last years of his life, under the stress of war and the desperate sense of urgency it gives to the creative artist who is threatened with annihilation by it, he had recovered the whole range of his inspiration over twenty years, so that he could resume and concentrate it in the new medium, the medium that was to give him immortality. There is a passage in *Beautiful Wales* which calls to mind at once the feeling in which so many of his poems are steeped:

So I came into a valley, and there was one white house in it, with a green, glowing and humming garden, and at the door a woman who might have been the Old Year. It was one of those white houses so fair that in the old times a poet compared a girl's complexion with them, as with lilies and foam. It held all the sun, so that suddenly I knew that in another valley, farther south and farther east, the rooks were making the lanes sleepy with their busy talk; the kingfishers were in pairs on the brooks, whose gentle water was waving and combing the hair of the river moss; the gold of the willow catkins was darkened by bees; over an old root of dock was a heaving colony of gleaming ants; perhaps the chiff-chaff had come to the larches and the little green moschatel was in flower with large primroses among the ash stools in wet woods; and in the splendid moments of the day the poplars seemed to come into the world, suddenly all purple. . . .

One could assemble a dozen passages from the poems in which one idea or another from that paragraph is echoed and transposed. The magic transmutations of the sun are one of Thomas's favourite themes; but more than anything else in nature rain seemed to have a mysterious power over him, bringing him his moments of intensest illumination:

Rain, midnight rain, nothing but the wild rain
On this bleak hut, and solitude, and me
Remembering again that I shall die

And neither hear the rain nor give it thanks
For washing me cleaner than I have been
Since I was born into this solitude.
Blessed are the dead that the rain rains upon:
But here I pray that none whom once I loved
Is dying tonight or lying still awake
Solitary, listening to the rain,
Either in pain or thus in sympathy
Helpless among the living and the dead,
Like a cold water among broken reeds,
Myriads of broken reeds all still and stiff,
Like me who have no love which this wild rain
Has not dissolved except the love of death. . . .

There are two famous passages about rain in the prose which this poem recalls. The first is in the early *South Country*:

At all times I love rain, the early momentous thunder-drops, the perpendicular cataract shining, or at night the little showers, the spongy mists, the tempestuous mountain rain. I like to see it possessing the whole earth at evening, smothering civilization, taking away from me myself everything except the power to walk under the dark trees and to enjoy as humbly as the hissing grass, while some twinkling house-light or song sung by a lonely man gives a foil to the immense dark force. I like to see the rain making the streets, the railway station a pure desert whether bright with lamps or not. It foams off the roofs and trees and bubbles into the water-butts. It gives the grey rivers a demonic majesty. It scours the roads, sets the flints moving, and exposes the glossy chalk in the tracks through the woods. It does work that will last as long as the earth. It is about eternal business. In its noise and myriad aspects I feel the mortal beauty of immortal things. . . .

The second, four years later in *The Icknield Way*, is more passionate and nearer the poetry:

I lay awake listening to the rain, and at first it was as pleasant to my ear and my mind as it had been long desired; but before I fell asleep it had become a majestic and finally a terrible thing, instead of a sweet sound and a symbol. It was accusing me and trying me and passing judgement. Long I lay still under the sentence, listening to the rain, and then at last listening to words which seemed to be spoken by a ghostly double beside me. He was muttering: the all night rain puts out summer like a torch. In the heavy black rain falling straight from the invisible dark sky the heat of summer is annihilated, the splendour is dead, the summer is gone. The midnight rain buries it away as it has buried all sound but its own. I am alone in the dark still night, and my ear listens to the rain piping in the gutters and roaring softly in the trees of the world. Even so will the rain fall darkly upon the grass over the grave when my ears can hear it no more. . . .

Such quotations inevitably provoke a challenge between the poetry and the prose; and precisely because Thomas's poetry keeps so close to the natural prose order of words in modern English, with the rhymes, assonances and internal rhymes happening as if by fortunate accident, and because the rhythms of the poetry are based on the rhythms of intimate conversation and letter-writing, there may seem at first very little to choose between them to anyone who responds to Thomas's feeling about the world: the man is whole, and what you love of his work in one medium, you will find to love in the other. Equally, however, Thomas's case defines more clearly than almost any other in our modern literature the superiority of poetry as the medium for the kind of thing that Thomas wanted to convey, which was not scientific analysis or rational argument or narration of fact, but emotion and intuition, the world of the senses' apprehension transformed by the light of imagination. It is the poetry that haunts the memory and burns itself into the deeper layers of our consciousness, by the incalculable power that basic poetic forms and the counterpointing of one rhythm against another in that concentrated field endow it with; and in making that judgement I am thinking of the best of the prose, not the passages in the early work which are marred by a rather whimsically mannered note, the fashion perhaps of their time.

The war years led me, as I believe they led a great many other people, to read Edward Thomas's poetry with a new attention, and to discover that it was standing up to the sorting of time and new circumstance quite extraordinarily well. Thomas only wrote one poem about the issues of the 1914 war. *This is No Case of Petty Right and Wrong* was not the kind of patriotic poem to please the mood of the early years of that war, nor was it a poem that voiced the bitter disillusionment that followed; it was a statement of cool, tolerant judgement and absolutely clear faith in the England he knew; a poem, in fact, that any young man of unmilitaristic sentiments without a political axe to grind could find sympathetic in 1939. It stands by itself, however, and the real reason for the power he seemed to radiate at that time lies in deeper and more general causes. In all his writing Thomas expressed the most profound melancholy; and the intensity of vision of which I spoke earlier, and which sets his poetry apart from the great mass of pleasing nature poetry which has been produced since Wordsworth, is also an intensity of suffering. Again and again he speaks of his delight in a landscape, the song of a bird, an old farm, or a mill stream, being crossed with pain, of scarcely knowing where the one emotion ends and the other begins. His melancholy is not that of languor or sensuousness, it comes from caring deeply about living things that meet misfortune or are destroyed before fulfilment, and it is haunted by their unhappiness even when the past in which he imagines them is a past still to come in the future:

> Now first, as I shut the door
> I was alone
> In the new house; and the wind
> Began to moan.
>
> Old at once was the house,
> And I was old;
> My ears were teased with the dread
> Of what was foretold,
>
> Nights of storm, days of mist, without end;
> Sad days when the sun
> Shone in vain: old griefs and griefs
> Not yet begun. . . .

If Thomas had written poetry at the beginning of his career I think one might well have found melancholy in it, because he had a temperamental propensity towards it; but not the melancholy of the actual poems he left us, which is a tragic melancholy, that is an awareness not only of the beauty and the possibility of success and happiness in our lives, but also of the inherent imperfection of the world that brings disaster in a new shape just when we have vanquished it in another, and makes our idealism the breeding-ground of our evil.

This tragic sense was bound to evoke a deep response in the disappointed hopes and sombre forebodings of 1939. But Thomas does not merely tell one poetically that grief always has been and will be again; he goes one step further. He is, it goes almost without saying, one of those writers who are only likely to emerge in an epoch when new knowledge and new possibilities in life cannot be fitted into the patterns established by the old religions and the conventional, time-hallowed systems of thought. Like Wordsworth, Thomas found in nature what other men in other ages found in religion; but there is, in his poetry, even less attempt than in Wordsworth's to construct a philosophical apology for this faith in nature. His aim is always the maximum of self-effacement: nature is to speak for herself as far as the medium of words can make it possible, and the imaginative experience is to be conveyed by that other dimension of poetry which resides in imagery, music and rhythm. So far, as a general rule, is he from attempting to rationalize or systematize his faith, that he is continually reaching towards an apprehension beyond words; he wants to think 'only with scents', he wants to use 'a language not to be betrayed' like birds and trees, and seizes his illumination in a chance appearance or word uttered by someone else, as in *The Brook*:

> A grey flycatcher silent on a fence
> And I sat as if we had been there since
> The horseman and the horse lying beneath
> The fir-tree-covered barrow on the heath,
> The horseman and the horse with silver shoes,
> Galloped the downs last. All that I could lose
> I lost. And then the child's voice raised the dead.
> 'No one's been here before' was what she said
> And what I felt, yet never should have found
> A word for, while I gathered sight and sound.

That is as far as he will go in the way of definition within a poem; but in *The South Country* which he published in 1909, he wrote:

> The landscape retains the most permanent marks of the past, and a wise examination of it should evoke the beginnings of the majestic sentiment of our oneness with the future and the past, just as natural history should help to give the child a sense of oneness with all forms of life. . . .

And again a few years later, describing an encounter with 'a man who had served twenty years imprisonment in a London office and was not yet done with it', and bitterly regretting the country life from which he was exiled, he wrote:

There was something firm and very mighty left even for him, though his melancholy, perverse temper could reach it only through memory. He had Nature to rest upon. He had those hills which were not himself, which he had not made, which were made for man and yet were good to him as well as to myriads of other races, visible and invisible, that have been upon the earth and in the air, or will be in some other moment of eternity. . . .

In those two passages are, I think, the key to the power of affirmation that such a melancholy and even despairing poet as Thomas communicates to us at a time when human beings are increasingly aware of being at the mercy of the artificial civilization that one side of their brain has created, and increasingly dislocated from a harmonious relation with the universe of which they are indissolubly part. Thomas's writing is steeped in the 'majestic sentiment of our oneness with the future and the past', in a 'sense of oneness with all forms of life', and that 'he had nature to rest upon' is perhaps the most perfectly appropriate epitaph one could imagine for the poet himself. And yet those phrases of his own are almost too magniloquent when applied to him. In his book on Richard Jefferies he said of his style:

There is not an uncommon word, nor a word in an uncommon sense, all through Jefferies' books. There are styles which are noticeable for their very lucidity and naturalness; Jefferies is not noticeable even to this extent. There are styles more majestic, more persuasive, more bewildering, but none which so rapidly convince the reader of its source in the heart of one of the sincerest of men.

Jefferies, he goes on to say, was often slipshod because he had no fine ear; but Thomas himself had a very fine ear indeed. In spite of this, much of what he says of Jefferies is true of his own case, and one can feel in his poetry a continual aspiration towards a lucidity and naturalness so complete that one would forget to be aware of it, an impulse to strip away all rhetoric and the slightest nuance of pretended emotion. In his pursuit of absolute naturalness and transparency he quickly found, with the example and encouragement of Robert Frost beside him, an individual style that creates the appropriate rhythmic shape for what he has to say. It is amazing to reflect that a man whose whole career in poetry only lasted from 1914 to 1917 was writing before his death poems such as *Words*, *Two Houses*, and *Out in the Dark*, which show a subjection of the medium to the imaginative ferment so complete that they are altogether new events in English poetry. It is equally amazing to remember that he had so much difficulty in placing them with editors at the outset; poems which are precious to us today, not for any deep intellectual probings or speculations, not for any brilliant dramatization of the predicament of our century, nor for even a single line consciously written in the grand manner, but for the passionate faith that underlies them in the elemental things from which our civilization—with a kind of implacable yet helpless momentum—is exiling us: in nature, in the rhythm of the seasons and birth and death, in the mystery of love and human personality, and that tragic sense of the past within the present:

But another house stood there long before:
And as if above graves
Still the turf heaves
Above its stones:
Dark hangs the sycamore,
Shadowing kennel and bones
And the black dog that shakes his chain and moans.

And when he barks, over the river
Flashing fast,
Dark echoes reply,
And the hollow past
Half yields the dead that never
More than half-hidden lie:
And out they creep and back again for ever.

But for Beaumont Hamel

Ever since the end of the 1914-18 war debate has continued about the respective merits of Rupert Brooke, the poet who expressed the eager, sacrificial mood of Britain when hostilities broke out; and Wilfred Owen, the poet of the dark end, when that crusading spirit had been irretrievably lost in the massacre and mud of northern France, to be replaced by something grimmer, more dogged and touched with desperation. Rupert Brooke has been attacked for falseness of emotion and superficiality by those who find in Wilfred Owen's sombre dirges the true voice of the modern civilized man turned soldier; and Wilfred Owen has been accused of defeatism by others who have feared the effect his disillusionment and whiplike satire might have on national morale.

In the middle of the last war—at a climax of violence in the fighting—I reviewed the works of both poets. Modern war imposes certain mass emotional checks that an individual escapes, is even conscious of only with the greatest difficulty. Nevertheless, I have found that the defeat of Germany and Japan has not altered the impression I received then.* But even under those circumstances it was possible to discern a certain confusion on both sides in the debate; for both Rupert Brooke and Wilfred Owen were great lovers of their country, and however unequal they may be in poetic power, both did a great service to their countrymen at the particular time they wrote. What is important to remember is that Wilfred Owen saw action, and action at its bloodiest and most horrible; Rupert Brooke, on the other hand, died of disease

* This essay formed the basis of a talk originally delivered on the overseas service of the B.B.C.

before he ever came into contact with the enemy. There is a passage in one of Wilfred Owen's letters that is worth much pondering. He was writing to a friend about a biography of Tennyson he had been reading in hospital just after his first return from France. The biography alleged that Tennyson was unhappy in spite of all his success and ease of life. 'I can quite believe', Owen writes, 'he never knew happiness for one moment such as I have—for one or two moments. But as for misery was he ever frozen alive with dead men for comforters? Did he ever hear the moaning at the bar, not at twilight and evening bell only, but at dawn, noon and night, eating and sleeping, walking and working, always the close moaning of the Bar; the thunder, the hissing and the whining of the Bar?—Tennyson, it seems, was always a great child. *So should I have been but for Beaumont Hamel.* Not before 1917 did I write the *only* lines of mine that carry the stamp of maturity —these:

> But the old happiness is unreturning
> Boys have no grief as grievous as youth's yearning;
> Boys have no sadness sadder than our hope. . . .

That happiness he had celebrated with a magic that is already entirely his own in one of the very few poems that survive from his writing before the war, those wonderful lines called *From My Diary*, written in July 1914, when he was twenty-one years old:

> Leaves
> Murmuring by myriads in the shimmering trees.
> Lives
> Wakening with wonder in the Pyrenees.
> Birds
> Cheerily chirping in the early day.
> Bards
> Singing of summer scything through the hay.
> Bees
> Shaking the heavy dews from bloom and frond.
> Boys
> Bursting the surface of the ebony pond.
> Flashes
> Of swimmers carving through the sparkling cold.
> Fleshes
> Gleaming with wetness in the morning gold. . . .

These lines are remarkable not only for the intense sensuous delight in the world which they reveal, but also for the experimenting with alliteration, onomatopoeia, internal rhymes and half rhymes, qualities which were to heighten so powerfully the effect of the later war poems. It is interesting to compare it with the famous poem by Rupert Brooke which also celebrated 'the old happiness'. *Grantchester* was written in Berlin in 1912 and is one of Rupert Brooke's most successful and popular poems; but I think it makes one feel—just as Wilfred Owen felt about Tennyson—that he was a great child. It is witty with a clever undergraduate wit, it shows a gay and delightful fancy, and an unperplexed enjoyment of nature, of that English countryside round Cambridge where this always fortunate and well-loved young man had spent some of his happiest years. And yet, if you compare it even with that poem by Wilfred Owen I have just quoted, and written before he reached his maturity, how much truer the emotion seems, how much more precise and telling the images Owen uses, how much more haunting the music he creates.

Rupert Brooke was to perform some astonishing virtuoso feats in poetry before he wrote the 1914 Sonnets by which he is most widely remembered. The impact of these Sonnets, with their fluency and colloquial novelty must have been very great when they first came out, though I was too young at the time to judge of that. But even a few years later, when they were put into my hands by an intelligent master at my private school, who could warn me at the same time of the way the conscripts of 1918 felt about them, they induced in me an almost giddy excitement of discovery. Today, as one looks back on them it is difficult not to feel that under the surface brilliance lies a corrupting glibness; not to find that though the fancy is charming, it too often supplies the place of imagination; not to want a little more passion instead of the all too facile sentiment, a more penetrating intellectual illumination sometimes instead of the ever-ready cleverness.

Rupert Brooke was never pedestrian; he could never have written if he had lived anything as humourless and flat as some of Wordsworth's poems of rustic life; but, equally, he could never have approached the imaginative intensity of even the simplest of Wordsworth's great poems, such as the *Highland Reaper*. Sometimes after reading him one is inclined to put the book down with the disappointed feeling that he is only a *poetic* writer, and not a poet at all; and then, suddenly, one comes on a passage of true lyrical grace and balance, as this from one of his Tahiti poems:

> *Tau here*, Mamua
> Crown the hair, and come away!
> Hear the calling of the moon,
> And the whispering scents that stray
> About the idle warm lagoon.
> Hasten, hand in human hand,
> Down the dark, the flowered way,
> Along the whiteness of the sand,
> And in the water's soft caress
> Wash the mind of foolishness,
> Mamua, until the day.
> Spend the glittering moonlight there
> Pursuing down the soundless deep
> Limbs that gleam and shadowy hair,
> Or floating lazy, half-asleep,
> Dive and double and follow after,
> Snare in flowers, and kiss and call,
> With lips that fade, and human laughter,
> And faces individual,
> Well this side of Paradise! . . .
> There's little comfort in the wise.

In many of his poems, Rupert Brooke wrote of death; and like greater poets before him, he wove some of his tenderest fancies around the idea. The *Sonnet* he wrote 'Suggested by some of the Proceedings of the Society for Psychical Research' is one of the most perfectly articulated of these:

> Not with vain tears, when we're beyond the sun,
> We'll beat on the substantial doors, nor tread
> These dusty high-roads of the aimless dead
> Plaintive for Earth; but rather turn and run
> Down some close-covered by-way of the air,
> Some low sweet alley between wind and wind,
> Stoop under faint gleams, thread the shadows, find
> Some whispering ghost-forgotten nook, and there
>
> Spend in close converse our eternal day;
> Think each in each, immediately wise;

Learn all we lacked before; hear, know and say
What this tumultuous body now denies;
And feel, who have laid our groping hands away;
And see, no longer blinded by our eyes.

This poem shows clearly enough how skilled he was in the art of making verses, and how felicitously he could—on occasion—as in the phrase 'tumultuous body'—choose his epithets. What promise, one feels inclined to say, will be fulfilled when this gift is moulded by mature experience. . . . And yet, as one reads on through the poems in which death is made the excuse for one fanciful reverie after another, one finds something almost pathetic in the way in which Brooke's mind sheers off the reality of the fact, refusing to face the terrors that lurk in death and suffering. Perhaps it is only between wars, or away from the theatres of war (and such Hesperides grow more and more remote and impossible with every fresh outburst of international slaughter), that these poems can ever be appreciated in the future as they were once. It is not for an imaginative realization of the inferno that is war that the 1914 Sonnets are famous, and it is of no searing ordeal, no doubt of what lies beyond the supreme sacrifice that *The Soldier* speaks:

If I should die think only this of me;
That there's some corner of a foreign field
That is for ever England. . . .

This sonnet, and the others that were published with it in 1915 may not have shown any conception of the darker side of the war, but they crystallized the mood of the time and gave it eloquent voice. By their vision of what the spirit of England meant, their romantic expression of the influences that shaped the lives of the young soldiers, under their most ideal light, of all the dreams of happiness to come that had to be abandoned as they went into battle, they gave comfort and encouragement to thousands whose brothers, sons and husbands had volunteered to stay the German onslaught. It was left to another poet who had ceased to be 'a great child'—because he had been in the fighting at Beaumont Hamel—to reveal the truth that Rupert Brooke did not, perhaps could not know, with all his mind and senses, the truth that war is terrible:

I have made fellowships—
Untold of happy lovers in old song.
For love is not the binding of fair lips
With the soft silk of eyes that look and long

By Joy, whose ribbon slips,—
But wound with war's hard wire whose stakes are strong
Bound with the bandage of the arm that drips;
Knit in the webbing of the rifle-thong.

I have perceived much beauty
In the hoarse oaths that keep our courage straight;
Heard music in the silentness of duty;
Found peace where shell-storms spouted reddest spate.

Nevertheless, except you share
With them in hell the sorrowful dark of hell,
Whose world is but the trembling of a flare,
And heaven but as a highway for a shell,

You shall not hear their mirth:
You shall not come to think them well content
By any jest of mine. These men are worth
Your tears. You are not worth their merriment.

That was written in November 1917 when Owen was only twenty-four, and only a little over three years later than *From My Diary*; but remarkable though that early poem was, what a swift maturing of the man and his power over words the new poem reveals. It is a poem, one can say, inconceivable in the poetic world of Rupert Brooke, with its solemn music rising from the depths of an experience in which agony and spiritual triumph were fused; an experience that had revealed the worthlessness of all the conventional martial enthusiasms and easy judgements of those who had never been 'where death becomes absurd and life absurder', but had taught in their stead a new passion of comradeship and endurance.

The stabbing realism of the images of war in this and the other poems written at the same time reflected not only a change in the nature of the war on the Western Front, which had settled down to a long struggle of attrition between enormous armies living under the foulest conditions imaginable, but also in the young poet's attitude towards his art. In the very first weeks following his arrival in France he had, as his letters show, grasped the beastliness underneath the inspiration of war. He had to see and endure things in the most shocking contrast to the life still existing on the English side of the Channel; and while he deliberately numbed himself to the shock, he determined that the people at home—and the generations of the future—must know this truth without the recognition of which patriotism would remain blind and evil. During those blood-soaked months of 1917 he learnt the deepest loathing for war; and when, invalided home in the late summer, a chance brought him the friendship of the older poet, Siegfried Sassoon, who was already known for his bitter attacks on those who were profiting materially or spiritually from the war, the conviction of what he had to do grew and hardened within him.

Later, when he had returned to France, he wrote to Sassoon: 'My senses are charred. I shall feel again as soon as I dare, but now I must not. I don't take the cigarette out of my mouth when I write Deceased over their letters. But one day I will write Deceased over many books.' That he now felt he had a mission to reveal and to warn, does not detract from the greatness of the poetry he was writing. He had trained himself too seriously as an artist ever to forget it. But he wanted it to be impossible for anyone to say of a poem he had signed 'How beautiful that is!' with a connoisseur's detachment only: to write pure poetry no longer had any meaning for him beside the sacred duty he felt to become the voice through which the agonies and wrongs of the men who were dying around him should be made known to the world. We should mistake Wilfred Owen as a human being if we were to forget this, and misjudge the sum total of what he has bequeathed to us; even though we may feel—indeed know—that it is only the greatness of the poetry that has preserved the message. In the *Preface* which he had already written to the book of his poems he never lived to complete or publish himself, he says explicitly: 'Above all I am not concerned with poetry. My subject is war, and the pity of war. The Poetry is in the pity. Yet these elegies are to this generation in no sense consolatory. They may be to the next. All a poet can do today is warn. That is why true poets must be truthful. If I thought the letter of this book would last, I might have used proper names; but if the spirit of it survives—survives Prussia—my ambition and those names will have achieved themselves fresher fields than Flanders. . . .'

Owen hated the 'spirit of Prussia' which had led to the obscene carnage; but like every courageous soldier gifted with imagination, he saw in the opponent facing him in battle only another suffering human being who must also have perceived, through the glare of the inferno to which they were both condemned, the same truth as he had. In one of his most memorable poems, where the hollow music created by his use of half-rhymes sounds at its most haunting, and in which he pictures a dream meeting between one soldier and the enemy he has killed, he expressed something that hundreds and thousands of fighting men have responded to in this war:

> . . . With a thousand pains that vision's face was grained
> Yet no blood reached there from the upper ground,
> And no guns thumped, or down the flues made moan.
> 'Strange friend,' I said, 'there is no cause to mourn.'
> 'None,' said the other, 'save the undone years,
> The hopelessness. Whatever hope is yours,
> Was my life also; I went hunting wild
> After the wildest beauty in the world,
> Which lies not calm in eyes, or braided hair,
> But mocks the steady running of the hour,
> And if it grieves, grieves richlier than here.
> For by my glee might many men have laughed,
> And of my weeping something had been left,
> Which must die now. I mean the truth untold,
> The pity of war, the pity war distilled.
> Now men will go content with what we spoiled.
> Or, discontent, boil bloody and be spilled.
> They will be swift with swiftness of the tigress,
> None will break ranks, though nations trek from progress.
> Courage was mine and I had mystery;
> Wisdom was mine, and I had mastery
> To miss the march of this retreating world
> Into vain citadels that are not walled. . . .

Wilfred Owen, who had distinguished himself as a leader of his men and had won the M.C. for one of his braver exploits, was killed on 4th November 1918, while superintending the crossing of the Sambre under heavy German machine-gun fire. Only one week more, and a poet would have been saved who had already shown himself capable as an artist of outdistancing almost all his contemporaries, and who held the utmost promise for the future of English letters. This thought makes the loss of such a precious life seem all the more bitter and futile; but he was spared the fulfilment of his prophetic poem. We do not know what Owen would have thought as Western Europe retreated into its 'vain citadels', nor how his profoundly pacific and humane spirit would have reacted when, in the vortex of that discontent which bred dictatorship, nations indeed trekked from progress—and, as he had foreseen, none broke ranks. . . . But if, when the hour struck again, the thinking young men of Britain went into war without illusions, with something of a recognition of the paradoxes that emerge even in the justest and most unavoidable war, and therefore with a temper far stronger than any brittle dreams of glory could impart, it was Wilfred Owen's poetry that had helped to create that temper. It is true that we can no longer feel as we felt at the beginning; a different war has made us different, and a great deal of what Owen said must strike us as historical, as belonging to a particular time and a tragic situation with other protagonists. The poetry of the last war, of the conscripted generation, at the rare points when it touched greatness, seemed to be the resolution of new, perhaps even more difficult problems of mind and spirit. At the same time it is impossible not to feel that Owen's work was a kind of touchstone or starting-place for them. How else could it be with the poet who wrote:

> But cursed are dullards whom no cannon stuns,
> That they should be as stones;
> Wretched are they, and mean
> With paucity that never was simplicity.
> By choice they made themselves immune
> To pity and whatever moans in man
> Before the last sea and the hapless stars;
> Whatever mourns when many leave these shores;
> Whatever shares
> The eternal reciprocity of tears.

A Greek Poet and His English Language

It is sometimes said, or lightly assumed, that poets and artists who die young, die at their appointed time, and that even if a prefiguring of their death is not to be found in their work, it clearly reveals that they had given the world all they had to give. There are, indeed, poets of whom this seems strangely true, and Shelley is one of them; but there are others, and Keats is one of them, of whom one can admit it only with the greatest difficulty. Their death appears wantonly to cut off a branch at the moment when it promised its most fruitful ripening. If Demetrios Capetanakis had lived, even if only for one or two more years, he would have been able to complete a cycle of work, already planned, which revealed itself more remarkable and beautiful with every advance he made.

He was only too conscious of this himself. It is true that, about eighteen months before his death, he had been passing through a crisis of despair, of agony of spirit for his own happiness and for the suffering of his country, and of doubt of his powers as an artist, which brought him to a point where he did not wish to live any longer. But what is remarkable is that, from this point, in spite of a severe attack of the illness that was eventually to kill him, he turned sharply back into a world of confidence and hope. He was happy, he said it again and again, and even when, in the winter before his death, he was once more too ill to get up, he contrasted his feeling of inner contentment then with the black mood in which the previous attack had found him. He was at work on the poems as long as his strength allowed him, even when it made him giddy and sent up his temperature to correct a single line; he still talked of the articles he intended to write, and for which he had taken elaborate notes; and when in the last few weeks he began to realize more clearly than his friends, who put the thought from them, that he might not recover, his constant preoccupation was with what he had not had time to do, what he still longed to contribute to the life of his time, perhaps even more in other ways, in action and personal teaching, than in literature.

He dreamed of writing a novel about London in wartime; he was eager to collaborate in a play, and a book about Shakespeare; those plans were for the future, but already, it seemed, within reach was a book of literary and philosophical criticism. The name he had thought of for it was *The Shores of Darkness*, a name which in itself, if one remembers the sonnet of Keats from which it is taken, implies hope. It was to consist of ten essays, with an introduction and conclusion. He had already written and published the essays on Rimbaud, Stefan George, Dostoevsky and the Notes on Contemporary Writers, though he thought of enlarging some of them, particularly the last. He had also written the essay on English poetry in its first form, and had allowed me to publish it in *Penguin New Writing*, though he never saw anything beyond the galley proofs; and the essay on Greek poetry had been delivered as a lecture, and, though unrevised, can be taken as substantially complete in the form in which it was published, including the wonderfully beautiful translations. Of the four other essays the first two were to be on Plato and Kierkegaard. He had thought for a very long time about these, and had indeed collected a small library of texts and reference books for the work. From the way he spoke about them to me and other friends, it is clear that he intended them to be as important as those he had already written, perhaps even more important. He was naturally modest about his work, but he was convinced that he had an original contribution to make to the understanding of Plato, and that no interpretation of Kierkegaard yet published in this country had reached the heart of his mystery. To my great sorrow, when I went through his papers after his death, I could find nothing of these two projected essays except the voluminous quotations he had copied out from the original works and the commentaries on them he had found most significant, and some fragments of earlier studies of these two philosophers, very closely argued and characteristic, but unfortunately in no state for publication. Everything was ready, but nothing was written. The loss to the world is, I am certain, no small one. Nor does anything survive of the essay on Friendship, which would have been one of his most eloquent if it contained anything of the enthusiasm and subtle learning he displayed when the theme was under discussion, or of The New World Quest, which was to have been devoted to the literature of the Americas in its most general aspects, and in particular to the novels of Thomas Wolfe in the United States and the critical writings of Eduardo Mallea in the Argentine. For these, there are not even notes to be found; only his carefully scored copies of the books show that they had already begun to take shape in his mind.

There were other articles and lectures among his papers, which were not intended for the book, but are of very great interest. Perhaps the most interesting is a lecture in French on Proust, a shorter version of an original study of considerable length, in which he analyses the way in which Proust, in the course of his book, continually alters his view about the individual, his anxiety about what can be grasped as real in life being the only constant. This I translated, and it was published in *New Writing and Daylight* (1945) for the first time. There is also a chapter of his unfinished study of Thomas Gray, concerned with Gray's relationship with Horace Walpole, and several lectures which he delivered officially as spokesman of Greece, and which brought him the applause of widely different audiences, and—what he especially prized in his last illness—an invitation to lecture after the war at London University. If he had lived I am certain he would also have written about the Spanish mystics, one of his favourite subjects, about many other aspects of French literature, and about Dickens. When he was unable to read anything else, even in his own language, he could still read Dickens: *Our Mutual Friend* was, I think, the last book he read before his death, and he found it, in his own phrase, 'a most wonderful book'.

Demetrios Capetanakis was a being of the rarest integrity in thought and feeling, and he was incapable of writing anything for the sake of 'making literature'. His integrity was even perhaps the cause of what may be thought to be a weakness in his work, a certain repetitiveness in argument and an excessive bareness of statement. These faults, if faults they are, arose from the strength of his passion to define, to grasp the inmost truth of his subject, whether an experience of his own, or the symbols, intellectual and imaginative, of another's experience. That passion was always with him; and the two forms of experience were always closely, indeed inextricably, associated with one another. The peculiar fascination of his studies of poets and philosophers lay in a combination of immense erudition and an unflagging curiosity about life, so that what he wrote out of his erudition had the excitement of something he might have lived through himself. In a sense he *had* lived through it, for being so passionately alive and sensitive in spirit, he had had overwhelming experiences of joy and terror, from which he had drawn certain conclusions about the nature of existence. His previous reading had helped him towards these conclusions; and once he had had the experience he looked back into his reading for corroboration; the tension of the resulting essay came from the thrill of discovering that the key seemed to fit, that sure enough the thread was leading him through the maze. To hold on to that thread was no easy task. He took immense care in the preparation of each essay, testing each fact as he fitted it into his argument, trying new words to capture something that had escaped the previous words; the effort was exhausting almost beyond the endurance of his frail physique. I do not believe that without astonishing courage and will-power he could have achieved so much during the months when his incurable illness, as we now know, had never really left him.

He intended to call his book *The Shores of Darkness*, because the conviction that grew ever stronger in him was that until one has become aware of the illimitable unknown that surrounds our lives, one cannot understand or properly value existence on earth. He judged artists and thinkers by the extent to which they revealed this awareness in their work. If they had never found themselves on the edge of an abyss where—

> Things which are not are destined to confound
> The things which are, the fortunes we have earned——

then he did not believe that we could learn much from them. Some authors, he would maintain, showed that no experience had ever come to them which caused them to question the nature of reality; others, whom he condemned above all, spent their lives concealing what had terrified them and turned their work into an elaborate unfertile pretence; but he believed that all that was significant in the European mind came from what he called philosophical anxiety. This thesis was already clearly stated in his first published study in English, on Rimbaud, in which the concluding words are: 'Nothingness might save or destroy those who face it, but those who ignore it are condemned to unreality. They cannot pretend to a real life, which if it is full of real risks, is also full of real promises.' As he went on, he began to formulate a view of English poetry, which he had intimately studied long before he came to Cambridge to write about Thomas Gray. It first appears in the essay on Stefan George. Seeing in George one of the chief spiritual corrupters of German youth, because his mind was 'too much of one piece to understand the dialectic mystery of existence, whose reality is born of nothingness, whose light comes from darkness, whose greatest hope is brought about by utmost despair,' he set out to define the fundamental error of 'state' poetry. In doing so he discovered that the greatest English poetry, though it was like George's poetry in the desire to make existence more solid, and unlike the poetry of such authors as Rilke which seems to dissolve the contours of experience, was fertile where George's was sterile because the desire came from a continual awareness of the limits of the known; because the English poets realized that, as he wrote in his essay on Dostoevsky, 'the more questionable everything appears, the more unquestionable the truth of something in man's existence, revealed by suffering and the awareness of nothingness becomes'. This was the idea that he developed in his essay on English poetry. It was, as he so often emphasized to me during his last illness, rather a series of introductory aphorisms than a connected study, which he intended to complete in the future. He was finding new things to interest and excite him in the English poets to the very end—I remember his enthusiasm about some passages of Blake, and Dryden's translations of Virgil of which he was reading an early eighteenth-century copy in bed—and anyone who heard him talk about his discoveries can only have the deepest regret for what he was unable to get down on paper. Above all one must regret the absence of a fuller study of Shakespeare: he gave only a hint of what he might have written in his few paragraphs on *Troilus and Cressida* in 'A View of English Poetry', though his Cambridge friends remember essays, since lost, which deeply impressed them.*

It was not only our serious poetry that aroused his wonder and delight. 'Although it sounds paradoxical,' he once wrote, 'it is true that comic verse is more apt than serious poetry to make us aware of the tragic side of our lives.' He applied to Lewis Carroll and Edward Lear the same test he had applied to Donne and Keats, and his friends in Cambridge remember how he used to quote:

> There was an old man who said 'Well!
> Will nobody answer this bell
> I have pulled day and night
> Till my hair has grown white,
> But nobody answers the bell.'

He dwelt on this limerick with intense enjoyment, but in the middle of his laughter would explain that it really was a profound metaphysical statement, and that the old man represented every poet or philosopher in his search for the truth about life. His gaiety and sense of humour do not appear very clearly in his published writings, though his fragment of a novel about Cambridge (written in Greek) is full of witty observation; but one could not be with him for long without discovering them. I can remember that when I was about to meet him for the first time, impressed by the reports of awed undergraduates that he had read *A la Recherche du Temps Perdu* through fourteen times, I expected someone of severe countenance and learned manner; it was an agreeable surprise to find a person entirely unassuming, full of fun, and ready to throw himself into any literary project that was on foot, if his friends appealed to him, with unreserved enthusiasm. He combined with this capacity for enthusiasm an extraordinary perceptive power, so that one found that what one wanted or what one needed was continually being anticipated before one had completely formulated it oneself, and one's intentions were always judged at their highest. It was this quality that made him the most stimulating of collaborators; it would be impossible for me to attempt to count how often I have profited from his sympathy and judgement.

* Some of these have only recently come to light.

It was also the genius he had for giving himself which made him so successful as a teacher of younger people. One of the happiest periods in his life was when he went up to the Midlands to help prepare a Friends' Ambulance Unit for relief work in Greece as soon as it was liberated. He made a deep impression on the young men, who learnt to read and write Greek extremely quickly under his guidance. That work of his is living now, in the restored freedom of his country which he so passionately longed to see.

There must have been moments when he felt very lonely, cut off from his country and family and knowing only that the most terrible things were a daily event under the German occupation; but he scarcely ever spoke of it, preferring to take part in the lives, the hopes and anxieties of his English friends. For England, after his violent revulsion from Germany and German philosophy, which for a time deeply influenced him during his studies at Heidelberg, and from the circle of Stefan George, he acquired a devotion and understanding that steadily increased, though he toyed intermittently with the idea of going to America; and he even thought of settling here for a long period after the war. His friend Panayotis Canellopoulos, once his University teacher and later War Minister of the exiled Greek Government, has written: '*Stefan George* was conquered by *Robinson Crusoe* and the poetry, or rather the life so miraculously without significance, of Thomas Gray. Scarcely had he arrived in Cambridge when he sent me two letters, in which he told me of these discoveries. In another letter he talked of John Donne and William Blake. He was cured.'

If there was no other evidence of his love for our country and civilization, his poems in English would be more than enough in themselves. No one who did not feel assimilated to our life in a supreme sympathy would have been capable of producing them. To me they are one of the most astonishing literary achievements I have ever come across. He was not always sure of certain words and phrases, and used to come to his English friends for advice, say, about the exact difference in a shade of meaning between two epithets; his vocabulary was not large though he was constantly increasing it, but in spite of this he seems to give the effect of ease and assured control of rhythm and idiom that are probably the most difficult secrets of all to conquer in a foreign language, even if one is already a poet.

His first serious attempt at writing English poetry was 'Detective Story' which appeared in *Penguin New Writing*. When he found it was a success he immediately began to plan more, and except during the times when illness prevented him, produced a slow but steady output. He was at work on several poems when he was taken to hospital, but destroyed nearly all these fragments; of the long poem on London there survive only one or two half-lines which were scattered among his notebooks, and a little more of another long poem on History. The first draft of one stanza of the latter gives an idea of what has been lost:

> No room in history is large enough
> To hold man's greatness. Even the most spacious
> Church is too small for all the hankering
> After eternity and love. . . .

And on another page, after many crossings out and rewritings, a clear—though by no means necessarily final—version of another stanza:

> Open the doors which History has shut
> And let the winds of uncreative passion
> Moaning outside the palace and the hut
> Blow in and break the walls of law and fashion. . . .

'Detective Story' has nearly all the qualities for which his poetry is remarkable: the direct and natural way in which he *spoke* in the four-line five-beat stanza, the intense dramatic, almost melodramatic situation conveyed so vividly and economically, and always behind it the metaphysical problem suggested with mystery and beauty. People were astonished by it, and disturbed; and that was exactly the effect he wanted to create. Poetry, he believed, must be disturbing before anything else, and because most people do not very much like being disturbed, or made to 'feel funny' in the phrase of Gertrude Stein he was fond of quoting, he did not find it at all surprising that true poetry is so often decried or ignored when it is first published.

I cannot, however, imagine anyone with a mind open to the action of poetry not being immediately disturbed and startled into recognition of a new imaginative experience by the first two stanzas of 'Abel':

My brother Cain, the wounded, liked to sit
Brushing my shoulder, by the staring water
Of life, or death, in cinemas half-lit
By scenes of peace that always turned to slaughter.

He liked to talk to me. His eager voice
Whispered the puzzle of his bleeding thirst,
Or prayed me not to make my final choice,
Unless we had a chat about it first.

And then he chose the final pain for me. . . .

Of this poem, Edith Sitwell has written in a remarkable passage:

> The voice that speaks to Abel is sometimes the voice of mankind speaking to the individual who must die that his brother may live—is sometimes the voice of democracy, the brotherhood that may fail us through sheer incomprehension. Sometimes it is the voice of the Statesmen of the world, hesitating on the brink of disaster . . . watching the play . . . waiting for the revelation which will solve the problem of the 'bleeding thirst'—the thirst that is the result of a wound. Surely there must be some explanation and way of healing? The sacrifice will not be necessary? But no explanation comes, and the poem ends with death inflicted on Man by his brother—the death that leads to freedom. Compared with this intensely strange poem, with its great profundity, leading us to the centre of the earth, the core of the heart, the central impulse from which thoughts and movements spring, many poems written by the stricken young of our time seem but surface poems.

Demetrios himself was contemptuous of work that had only a surface charm, and saw through any involved pretence of being subtle or profound; but if poetry startled by some sharp new vision in which he could find a deeper symbolism, or betrayed philosophical anxiety, then he was ready to forgive even serious technical weaknesses. I think it would be true to say that he never read a poem unless he had read *through* it first. He was always on the lookout for the meaning behind the poem, however concealed the expression and however unconscious the author himself might be of what he was really expressing. It was the same with music of which he was very fond; one evening at a performance of Tschaikowsky's *Swan Lake* he exclaimed, with characteristic abandon, that

Act II was the most haunting thing he had ever heard, because of the questioning of life, a questioning that is never answered, which he found in the music.

His own poems were fashioned directly out of his experience, but it would be a mistake to read them too literally in that sense. He had such a strong instinct for the dramatic, that there is in nearly every poem that might be read as autobiography a deliberate fusion of the imagined with the real. What was important for him was to make of them 'cryptic messages', 'with hints of what to hope and how to live', and under their surface simplicity the messages are often not at all easy to decipher. The difficulty is increased because, with his great knowledge of European thought, it came naturally to him to introduce references, in phrase or image, to the ideas of Plato, or San Juan de la Cruz, or Kierkegaard, or another philosopher. Always the thought and suffering of Europe was with him, in that perspective of three thousand years since his own nation had laid the first foundations of our civilization, and in them he saw a dominant conception of human life emerging from experiences repeated again and again under changing forms. It was this that gave such force to his interpretation of individual writers, that made him see many of our own writers, such as Thomas Gray or Dickens, in a quite unexpected and revealing light, and that showed up so much of what passes for criticism today in England as shallow and parochial by comparison. He did not reject the chief interpretative instrument of our time, psycho-analysis—he was too much entertained by its results—but he held that, in his own words, 'psychology can explain things, but it never reveals their meaning'.

When it became clear to him that he might never finish the long poems on which he had embarked, he abandoned them and summoned all his remaining strength to write the two pieces which must be considered his testament, 'The Isles of Greece' and 'Lazarus'. He had spoken more than once about his desire to write a poem presenting a truth about Greece which Byron had missed in his famous poem; and now, into those twenty short lines he distilled all that he felt about his country and her eternally renewed destiny of suffering, lines which are among the most tragic and haunting he ever wrote, and which express Greece perhaps more completely than anything that has been written in our time. One verse alone seems to me to concentrate and contrast with almost incredible force the symbols of outward and inward agony:

> The dusty fig-tree cries for help,
> Two peasants kill one snake,
> While in our rocky heart the gods
> Of marble hush and break. . . .

This poem we discussed together several times before his death, and the version which has been published received his final approval. The other, 'Lazarus', which I find more mysterious and more disturbing than all his other poems, even the supremely beautiful 'Abel', he did not want published. He felt that it was full of ambiguities and could have been much improved if he had had time to work on it. Nevertheless I am certain that if he had lived I could have persuaded him to reverse his decision, and after some heart-searching I decided that those lines, formed from the deepest spiritual experiences of his last years of life, and referring unmistakeably to the crisis of the winter of 1942-3 when he all but died, should belong to the world. I quote them here in full:

> This knock means death. I heard it once before
> As I was struggling to remember one,
> Just one thing, crying in my fever for
> Help, help. Then the door opened, yet no Son
>
> Came in to whisper what I had to know.
> Only my sisters wetted me with tears,
> But tears are barren symbols. Love is slow,
> And when she comes she neither speaks nor hears:
>
> She only kisses and revives the dead
> Perhaps in vain. Because what is the use
> Of miracles unheard of, since instead
> Of trying to remember the great News
>
> Revealed to me alone by Death and Love,
> I struggled to forget them and become
> Like everybody else? I longed to move
> As if I never had been overcome

By mysteries which made my sisters shiver
As they preparéd the supper for our Friend.
He came and we received Him as the Giver,
But did not ask him when our joy would end.

And now I hear the knock I heard before,
And strive to make up for the holy time,
But I cannot remember, and the door
Creaks letting in my unambiguous crime.

There was also a handful of other poems among his papers, most of which he had read over to me before he went to hospital, and which I therefore felt no hesitation in publishing with the rest in the memorial volume *A Greek Poet in England*. There are passages of startling beauty in 'Guilt', 'Angel', 'Experienced by Two Stones', 'Friendship's Tree' and 'A Song for Bores', all of them containing expressions of his central philosophical ideas, and 'American Games' is particularly interesting in the light of his enthusiastic curiosity about the American mind and character; but I think it is important to remember in reading these poems, that he might have made changes if he had had a chance to revise them for publication.

He died in Westminster Hospital on 9th March 1944 of incurable leucaemia. He was thirty-two years old. Many emergency treatments, even operations, had been tried, some of them very painful, but nothing made any difference for more than a few hours. The day before his death I had gone in to see him in the early evening, and sat beside his bed, fighting against the acceptance of what his grey and hollow face unmistakeably told me. He had beside him an enormous apple, which my mother had sent him from her garden. 'I have been eating it all day,' he said to me. 'It's the most wonderful apple.' In fact very little of it had been consumed, as he had at that last stage neither the energy nor the appetite, but he held it as if it symbolized for him the warmth and fullness of summer and the richness of the earth's fruits, all the things he knew he was being deprived of for ever.

He was buried in the Greek cemetery at Norwood, where so many of his distinguished compatriots who came to live amongst us—and how numerous they have been—lie in their crowded sepulchres towards the top of the gently rising slope, under the shadow of a Greek temple. On his gravestone are carved the lines from Donne which had always moved him so much:

> I am rebegot
> Of absence, darkness, death, things which are not!

Below them is a beautiful quotation from a Greek folk-dirge, chosen by a younger poet and countryman also living in England, Nanos Valaoritis:

*τιὰ δες καιρὸ πού διαλεξες χὰρε μου νὰ τον πὰρης**

In a brief, but deeply affectionate and perceptive reminiscence, William Plomer has spoken of his 'dark eyes, glowing with intelligence and feeling', of his slight build and 'delicate, nervous hands of an almost Asiatic fineness', and the 'fine smooth forehead and clear skin' that gave his face its remarkable harmony and sculptured radiance, though there was nothing in it of Praxitelean beauty. But there was a quality in his features, above all in the expression given by the mouth, which did, increasingly as one got to know him, recall an earlier phase of Greek sculpture. No one has described it better than Panayotis Canellopoulos:

> My friend's smile: one can only say that it was an archaic smile. Egyptian Pharaohs, Greek archaic statues, Etruscan gods—do not all those strange countenances seem to belong at the same time to childhood and to an impossible kind of maturity? It was almost the same feeling that my friend's face gave me. Often, while looking at it, I felt that I was like someone who has to unravel an impossible problem. And the impossible is life itself. I would look at my friend's face, and an even graver conviction would come to me: that death itself is what is impossible.

* What a season, O Death, you chose to take him away.

A Human Standpoint

The first thing I knew of Alun Lewis's death was when I was rung up from the editorial offices of a daily newspaper, and asked if I could write a short obituary note. The news was a great shock to me, and I found it quite impossible to say anything then and there. Up to that moment the war had seemed miraculously to spare the young English writers and artists whose work I most believed in; but in that moment I knew there were going to be no miracles, and my mind was trapped in a miserable foreboding. But I was also embarrassed by the newspaper's request, because I had never met Alun Lewis, though we had corresponded for several years, and I was critical of him as a poet, though I had published several of his poems.

I still feel something of the same embarrassment, because Alun Lewis had many friends who knew him intimately and loved him, and many who had never met him loved his poetry with an unqualified enthusiasm I could never muster. To all those I offer my apologies for writing as I shall in these pages, but it would be wrong of me to pretend that I thought he was comparable in his poetic achievement with Edward Thomas or Wilfred Owen, the victims of an earlier war, and his own admired masters, or even with some of his own contemporaries who survived the war. It would be unfair to those survivors as well as insincere, because death in battle does not by some mysterious magic immediately make a young man a better poet. But I do think the war, not the bullet that killed him, made Alun Lewis a writer: a writer who was capable of very big things indeed. I had read his volume of stories *The Last Inspection* with the feeling that prose, not verse, might turn out in the end to be his proper medium; and when he sent me from India his story *Ward O 3 (b)*, which is still to me one of the most brilliant stories written by anyone during the war, this feeling became a conviction. Alun Lewis knew I felt that way about his work, but it didn't offend him, and I think he was as sorry as I was that his posting to India prevented our meeting. In a letter he wrote to me just before embarkation, he said 'My job looks like being fast, violent and very technical. I contemplate it vaguely just at the present through a haze of farewells, one of which, although I've never met you, I hereby send to you.'

That letter and the tragedy that followed, sent me on a quest to discover glimpses of him from his friends and those who had been nearest to him at various times in his life. From what they have written to me, as I shall show, I have been able to form some pictures for myself of the features of the poet I shall always regret not having talked with or known personally; and nothing in them has contradicted the impression his writing had already given me.

Alun Lewis left us two books of poems, *Raider's Dawn* and *Hat Ha! Among the Trumpets*, the volume of stories I have just referred to, and a posthumous collection (*In a Green Tree*) consisting of letters—originally published as *Letters from India*, selected by his widow—together with his last stories, including *Ward O 3 (b)* and the almost equally remarkable *The Orange Grove*. I have just read all these again, and I am more than ever impressed by a quality that runs right through them, a natural human warmth, but also something more than that. There is a passage in the long poem, the last he ever wrote and perhaps the best, called *The Jungle*, which expresses it very beautifully:

> Some things we cleaned like knives in earth,
> Kept from the dew and rust of Time,
> Instinctive truths and elemental love,
> Knowing the force that brings the teal and quail
> From Turkestan across the Himalayan snows
> To Kashmir and the South alone can guide
> That winging wildness home again. . . .

It is this sureness about the things that matter, above all love, this rootedness in life and faith in the sensual world that seem to me so important about Alun Lewis. One of the reasons for this sureness may well have been the unusually happy childhood and home life that he had experienced. He was the eldest of a family of four, with two brothers and a sister, who all adored one another and reciprocated equally their parents' love for them. In a letter to me his mother has written:

As a family we seem to have laughed our way through the years between the wars. Money was never sufficient to supply all our family's needs, and they knew that scholarships had to be the order of the day. But if they worked hard, they played hard too, and tennis, hockey, swimming, hiking, rugger were their enthusiastic pastimes. Then there were those Bohemian holidays in secluded Penbryn, to pay for which my husband did extra evening work; and when we played and laughed, swam, read and lazed to our heart's content, and when, in looking back, the sun seems always to have been shining, the sky and sea blue and the sand shimmering gold.

In the same letter his mother also reveals another point of no little significance: that she had always wanted to be a writer, and that his becoming a writer had been felt to be an affair in which the two of them were specially and intimately associated. 'One day when he was about fifteen', she recalls, 'he came hurriedly into the house from one of his solitary strolls on the mountains, calling excitedly to me: "Look, Mother, I can do it." And he showed me five short poems that had come to him on the mountain top. One was *Five Silver Birches* to be seen in *Raiders' Dawn*, another was *Vanité* published by *The Sunday Times* soon afterwards. . . .'

This belief in life and the touchstone of the heart, qualities, it is worth remembering, that made Wordsworth a great poet, are all too rare today, when literature in so many countries is in danger of being dominated by pseudo-philosophies and the ingenious constructions of the intellect that really deny the heart; and this makes Alun Lewis's death particularly tragic for us. He was always striving to express his faith and vision more clearly and completely in his art, and in one of his letters he says:

I find my memory, in my 29th year, is taking a new and definite shape to itself. It's discarding everything it doesn't need to write and dream upon. It retains the bare necessities of soldiering: otherwise it forgets. All the stuff I learnt at College and Pengam has gone by the board, and it tunes itself more and more to the simple human material of life and of itself. It won't even acquire the economic statistics of the Beveridge Report, newspaper articles or Oxford pamphlets. It's going native, quite definitely and all its reasoning is done from a human standpoint. My longing is more and more for one thing only, integrity, and I discount the other qualities in people far too ruthlessly if they lack that fundamental sincerity and wholeness. So I only hope that I will be able to write, for I'm sure I won't be able to do anything else half as well.

Alun Lewis may have felt that the best part of him went into his writing, that secret soul he kept inviolable from the life of a soldier; but soldiering is not merely marching and shooting, it is relationships with other soldiers, and about that Lewis really cared. I have had testimony from many of his fellow writers who were in close contact with him at one point or other during his army career, and all tell the same story. 'He was a quiet, undemonstrative man,' says Jack Aistrop who was with him in the early days of the war at a big R.E. camp in the south, 'and once he had accepted one as a friend, quieter still. But with some strangers he would be awkward and extremely shy. He was practical and always knew what he wanted and the best way to get it. . . . And despite his quietness he had great store of energy. This energy was largely used in fighting against the stupid things of army life, and he was a thorn in the side of visiting lecturers and brass-hats. If they made stupid remarks a lone figure would invariably get to his feet and launch polite but scathing questions. . . .' Another fellow-writer, who met him a little later, Julian Maclaren-Ross, has also described this shyness and his contempt for 'the stupid things of army life', especially when it prevented sympathy between man and man even if one man was an officer and the other a soldier in the ranks. Maclaren-Ross also noted as a dominant trait his 'deep tenderness towards life itself', and his nostalgia for the elemental simplicities of his Welsh home. This nostalgia saturates many of his early poems and stories: it was so strong an emotion that it was a long time before he got it under control in his art—but he did get it under control, as *Ward O 3 (b)* is there to witness, with its beautiful balance of satiric observation and warm human insight, and what I can only call a kind of poetic wisdom transmuting the violent feelings that his theme must have had for him. At the time when he wrote this story, the last few months of his life, he seems indeed to have travelled far towards the attainment of that 'wholeness' he speaks about in the letter. Since his death, many people have told me they agree that *Ward O 3 (b)* is his masterpiece, and that they are as certain as I am that prose would have been his master-medium; and I have been particularly interested to find his mother—though she believed that, given the chance, he might have excelled in drama, poetic or non-poetic—among them. In the letter from which I have already quoted, she says:

> Prose was to be his major work. I know it by the same intuitive process as I knew he was going to be a writer. Generally speaking, his poems came to him too easily, out of the blue; though I knew there were exceptions, with which he wrestled in the black silences as Jacob struggled with the Angel. But in his prose, he had the joy and pride of the true craftsman. Often he refers to it in his letters, always as his future life's task. Of the story of a British battalion on foreign service, which he had in his mind on entering the Arakan, he wrote: 'I will give you bigger fruit than ever came out of the Orange Grove.'

It is impossible justly to compare the young British writers who were lost in the Second World War—and Alun Lewis in my opinion is one of them most bitterly to be regretted, together with Sidney Keyes and Dan Billany—with those who were mourned in 1918. Promise can always be interpreted in so many ways, is always so obscure in relation to events that had not been foreseen; and the writers of the First World War had different spiritual fronts to wage their war on. Nevertheless, even though I feel almost certain that *as a poet*—that is in the medium of verse—Alun Lewis was not and would not have been the peer of Wilfred Owen, there are many points of similarity in the total personalities of the two soldier writers. And one of them is their sense of comradeship and identity with their men. Bernard Gutteridge describes Lewis as follows:

> He was Intelligence Officer in the regiment and quite obviously efficient and extremely popular. He was one of those rare, quiet, sympathetic people whom one met as officers in the army who were both good officers and well-loved. . . . He was called 'our poet' throughout his brigade in a thoroughly affectionate way—and that says a lot, I think. . . . Incidentally, he could have got promotion and a safer job months before, but was absolutely insistent that he should go into action with the boys.

Alun Lewis refers in more than one letter to this feeling about not being separated from his men. It was something more complex than liking and the sense of human trust. He says in one place:

'I'm frightened of leaving them. They seem to have some secret knowledge that I want and will never find out until I go into action with them and war really happens to them. I dread missing such a thing, it seems desertion to something more than either me or them.' In his story *The Orange Grove*, he says of one of his characters: 'He was experiencing one of those enlargements of the imagination that come once or perhaps twice to a man, and re-create him subtly and profoundly. . . .' Such an enlargement of the imagination came to Alun Lewis, I feel sure, in India. It was a disturbing experience, too, rather like that sudden sense of 'unknown modes of being' that came to the boy Wordsworth when he was rowing across Ullswater. Only it was complicated for Alun Lewis by the *sky* of India, the sense, as E. M. Forster has described it, that 'outside the arch there seemed always another arch, beyond the remotest echo a silence'. And in this experience the categories of thought and value which he had accepted in his youth, in England, seemed gradually to be losing their meaning, to be swallowed up in something vaster. Here again his last poem *The Jungle* gives us clues:

> But we who dream beside this jungle pool
> Prefer the instinctive rightness of the poised
> Pied kingfisher deep darting for a fish
> To all the banal rectitude of states,
> The dew-bright diamonds on a viper's back
> To the slow poison of a meaning lost
> And the vituperation of the just. . . .

Alun Lewis was lost, like Staff-Captain Beale in *The Orange Grove*, driving on and on through the unknown landscape with his dead driver in the back of his truck—an image that has always reminded me of Yeats's lines about the soul 'sick with desire and fastened to a dying animal'. The whole story indeed is like a parable of the spiritual experience that Alun Lewis was going through. It is the gipsies who rescue Captain Beale when his truck finally sticks in the river bed, people he cannot understand, going in a direction he cannot guess, but elemental, smiling, and guided by some secret certainty. 'He wished, though, that he knew where they were going. They only smiled and nodded when he asked. Maybe they weren't going anywhere much, except perhaps to some pasture, to some well.' Those are the last sentences of *The Orange Grove*. And if Alun Lewis was lost in one sense to 'the banal rectitude of states', he still had with him the 'instinctive truths and elemental love' that he had kept 'cleaned like knives in earth', and the presentiment that he was on the verge of discovering something far greater than he had lost. All his hints about the search for integrity, and reasoning only from a human standpoint, and the bonds with the men under his command which he found so difficult to analyse, are pointers to that, and pointers too to the role he might have played in literature if he had lived. But there was a sense of darkness also, and it invades the last lines of *The Jungle*:

> A trackless wilderness divides
> Joy from its cause, the motive from the act;
> The killing arm uncurls, strokes the soft moss;
> The distant world is an obituary,
> We do not hear the tappings of its dread.
> The act sustains, there is no consequence,
> Only aloneness, swinging slowly
> Down the cold orbit of an older world
> Than any they predicted in the schools,
> Stirs the cold forest with a starry wind,
> And sudden as the flashing of a sword
> The dream exalts the bowed and golden head
> And time is swept with a great turbulence
> The old temptation to remould the world.
> The bamboos creak like an uneasy house;
> The night is shrill with crickets, cold with space.
> And if the mute pads on the sand should lift
> Annihilating paws and strike us down
> Then would some unimportant death resound
> With the imprisoned music of the soul
> And we become the world we could not change?
> Or does the will's long struggle end
> With the last kindness of a foe or friend?

That poem reached England after he was dead. For the annihilating paws struck only too soon. He was out on patrol in the Maya Hills, following a difficult and dangerous path. Then the fatal accident occurred: we are told that he slipped on a stone, and the loaded revolver he was carrying went off, mortally wounding him.

A stupid accident, one might say on hearing such a piece of news and knowing nothing of the persons involved, just the kind of thing that happens in a war. . . . But, whatever happened in that still mysterious episode, the person happened to be a young writer whose fame, even on the slender remains of his work we have, has already spread to many countries, and will continue to spread and grow as his 'cryptic message' expands and sinks itself in our hearts.

The Poet in the Modern World*

It may seem to you rather strange to feel very deeply, to want to talk about the position of the poet, the imaginative creator, in the modern world: almost as if I proposed to discuss the position of a leaf in an autumn gale. For indeed, to most of us, looking round on the devastated world the recent war has left behind it, the bomb-shattered towns, the families stricken by death or disease, the dislocated national economies, the blasted hopes of the young and the ruined lifetime's labours of their parents, reflecting on all this chaos and misery and knowing that the forces which caused it are capable of even greater and more cruel destruction at any time in the future, the work of the poet may seem of quite infinitesimal importance. I sometimes feel like that myself; and it is as if I saw the leaves of the volumes of Dante, of Shakespeare, of Goethe, torn and rain-sodden and blowing far away into the storm, as if I heard the voices of the poets of our own time, of Rainer Maria Rilke, William Butler Yeats, Federico Garcia Lorca and many others who are still alive, struggling in vain against the howling of the wind, and finally silenced. That is in moments of black pessimism; but such extreme moods are bad guides to the real state of affairs, and when they ebb, as they always do, I feel certain that the truth lies elsewhere. Then, not in Plato's divine frenzy, but with as careful judgement as I can muster, with experience testing intuition and the witness of what some of the greatest minds of the past have held to be true, I am prepared to assert that so far from poetry being without power or value in the modern world—that is, precisely, in the lives of you and me today in the fifth decade of the twentieth century—it is one of the very few things which can save us from the ultimate

* A lecture delivered at Vienna, 1947.

catastrophe that threatens our civilization, perhaps the only thing in the long run. I am not talking of miracles; for tomorrow and the day after we depend on the exertions of statesmen, who sometimes blunder into wise actions, to build the dykes and defences; but behind those walls the poet's work can be accomplished to restore those more permanent defences which may turn back evil if it comes.

When I declare such a faith, I am not making any very revolutionary statement. I am only reaffirming what has been said, in my country for one, on many occasions in the past. It was nearly three-quarters of a century ago that an English poet, one in whom the imaginative and critical faculties were most equally balanced, Matthew Arnold, said:

> The future of poetry is immense, because in poetry, when it is worthy of its high destinies, our race, as time goes on, will find an ever surer and surer stay. There is not a creed which is not shaken, not an accredited dogma which is not shown to be questionable, not a received tradition which does not threaten to dissolve. Our religion has materialized itself in the fact, in the supposed fact, and now the fact is failing it. But for poetry the idea is everything; the rest is a world of illusion, of divine illusion. Poetry attaches its emotion to the idea; the idea is the fact. The strongest part of our religion today is its unconscious poetry.

I do not think anyone will want to deny that the state of affairs which disturbed Matthew Arnold so deeply in the seventies of the nineteenth century has got worse since his day. If every creed seemed to be shaken then, most of them are lying half in ruins today, and the attacks on those ruins do not cease; and if all received traditions appeared to him to be dissolving, many of them have altogether vanished out of sight in our own times, so that we may truly feel sometimes that all the wisdom the present can gather from the past is nothing but a 'heap of broken images', as in that memorable passage from T. S. Eliot's *The Waste Land*:

> What are the roots that clutch, what branches grow
> Out of this stony rubbish? Son of man,
> You cannot say, or guess, for you know only
> A heap of broken images, where the sun beats,
> And the dead tree gives no shelter, the cricket no relief
> And the dry stone no sound of water. . . .

When Matthew Arnold wrote, the tide of prosperity which those tremendous developments in science and the technique of production we call the Industrial Revolution brought to all Europe and America, and particularly to my own country, was still rising; it required a very clear and penetrating vision to discern the spiritual danger so far ahead as he did. And yet he was indeed only elaborating what the poet Shelley had said half a century before, in the aftermath of the Napoleonic Wars:

> The cultivation of poetry is never more to be desired than at periods when, from an excess of the selfish and calculating principle, the accumulation of the materials of external life exceed the quantity of the power of assimilating them to the internal laws of human nature. The body has then become too unwieldy for that which animates it. . . . Poetry redeems from decay the visitations of the divinity in man. . . .

Here, then, are two unequivocal claims, by two first-class minds, both poets and critics, one speaking three-quarters of a century ago and the other over a century ago, that in times precisely such as we live in, when every compass by which man has steered himself through the long voyage of history seems to fail, when those who look for the clue of order in the deepening chaos of the world around them are like travellers who might appeal to the oracle among the weed-grown ruins of modern Delphi—in such times poetry alone can answer and provide. 'Poetry', says Shelley, 'redeems from decay the visitations of the divinity in man.' If we are to be convinced by his whole thesis we must understand what he means by this mysterious and pregnant utterance. It is perhaps in the works of the great Swiss historian Jakob Burkhardt that we find the most brilliant annotation, as it were, to Shelley's statement. In his *Reflections on History* Burkhardt says:

> Unsatisfied with mere knowledge, the domain of the specialized sciences, aware of its multiform, enigmatic nature, the human mind feels that there are still other powers which respond to its own obscure impulses. It comes to realize that great worlds surround it which speak only in images to the images it bears within it—the worlds of art. To the representation of those worlds it will infallibly attribute greatness, since it owes them the increase of its own most inward essence and power. For they are able to embrace nearly the whole of man's existence wherever it rises above the daily round, to express his state of mind in a much higher sense than he could himself, to grant him a transfigured image of

the world which, cleared of the débris of the contingent, gathers into itself only what is great, significant and beautiful. Even tragedy is then consoling. The arts are a faculty of man, a power and a creation. Imagination, their vital central impulse, has at all times been regarded as divine. . . .

And if we then turn back to Shelley, we shall find that there is another passage in *The Defence of Poetry* which most appositely illuminates the operation of this 'vital central impulse, imagination:

> Ethical science arranges the elements which poetry has created, and propounds schemes and proposes examples of civil and domestic life: nor is it for want of admirable doctrines that men hate, and despise, and censure, and deceive, and subjugate one another. But poetry acts in another and diviner manner. It awakens and enlarges the mind itself by rendering it the receptacle of a thousand unapprehended combinations of thought. . . . The great secret of morals is love; or a going out of our nature, and an identification of ourselves with the beautiful which exists in thought, action, or person not our own. A man, to be greatly good, must imagine intensely and comprehensively; he must put himself in the place of another and of many others; the pains and pleasures of his species must become his own. The great instrument of moral good is the imagination; and poetry administers to the effect by acting upon the cause. Poetry enlarges the circumference of the imagination by replenishing it with thoughts of ever new delight, which have the power of attracting and assimilating to their own nature all other thoughts, and which form new intervals and interstices whose void forever craves fresh food. Poetry strengthens the faculty which is the organ of the moral nature of man, in the same manner as exercise strengthens a limb. . . .

At this point I want to make it quite clear that I do not narrow poetry, the poetry through which imagination works, only to what is written in metre and rhyme. The subject is too large to develop here, and it would take me too long to explain why I believe that, though metrical form is essential to poetry's supreme manifestations, a great deal of prose has more in it of poetry than many a careful exercise in metre. I think, however, that I shall meet with general agreement if I say that in considering poetry in the sense I have chosen today we must include such prose as Adalbert Stifter and Rainer Maria Rilke wrote in your language, and John Donne, Thomas de Quincey and Virginia Woolf wrote in mine.

There remains also another point to be cleared up. The action of art, of poetry is not always the same in all ages. There have been imposing civilizations and long-enduring epochs when art was only the servant and flatterer of an established religion and a rigidly defined social order. In such epochs religion and state answered all questions and defined all experiences both in this world and beyond the grave. Such, we are led to believe, was the condition of Ancient Egypt and such, in its most fortunate heyday, the medieval Christian world. It is only when political collapse, alien gods or revolutionary knowledge destroy the basis of such societies that poetry comes into its own, as the stars remain to guide the sailor when charts and compasses have been swept overboard.

In the passage I have already quoted, Matthew Arnold said: 'Our religion has materialized itself in fact, in the supposed fact, and now the fact is failing it.' By that I take it that he meant that the spiritual truth and beauty which is the essential inspiration of Christianity, and something altogether unassailable, had been built into a wonderful complete structure of dogma, knowledge and conduct—the medieval world view—which answered all questions until the new knowledge of the modern world brought the whole structure toppling to the ground—and with it all that was really true and beautiful in it.

That earthquake occurred in the Renaissance; and we have been enduring the after-tremors of it ever since. One would imagine, if Arnold and Burckhardt are right, that after its first impact a tremendous counter-effort of the creative imagination to re-establish order on a new basis, on the basis of poetry, would emerge. And that, I believe, did occur, in the person of the greatest poet of Western civilization, William Shakespeare. From the very first Shakespeare was held to be a supremely natural writer, a writer, that is, whose works reflected life as one really experienced it, and not as one was taught it or expected to view it; and one of his earliest and most famous critics, the poet John Dryden said: 'He was the man who of all modern, and perhaps ancient poets, had the largest and most comprehensive soul. All the images of nature were still present to him, and he drew them not laboriously, but luckily: when he describes anything you more than see it, you feel it too.' Again and again we find this idea repeated in subsequent criticism; but it was not until fairly recent times that the attempt was made to relate Shakespeare's achievement to the background of philosophy and science in his time, to the Elizabethan, the English Renaissance vision of the world. Modern scholars have made it clear that Shakespeare lived at a crucial moment for the intellectual and spiritual development of Western civilization; the old, medieval conception of the universe, had suffered irreparable damage when Galileo confirmed the theories of Copernicus in cosmology, when Montaigne quietly took man off the pedestal on which for centuries accepted thought had placed him, and Machiavelli challenged the assumptions of political morality which had been inherited from Cicero. The whole so perfectly balanced edifice of ideas by which the Western world had lived for so long collapsed, as a dome collapses when you blow up the key pillars which support it. One of the immediate results was the split between science and morality, the dire effects of which we are still suffering from. As the distinguished American scholar, Theodore Spencer, has said:

> Bacon, taking, as he thought, all knowledge for his sphere, was the forerunner of those people who, down to our own day, have proclaimed the importance of knowledge for the sake of knowledge alone—people who have at the same time unconsciously sanctioned the irresponsible development of practical machinery and invention. Bacon was one of the first representatives of that split between knowledge and morality, which has had such enormous consequences for our civilization. . . .

It was out of this situation that Shakespeare created his masterpieces. He had neither an accepted religion nor an accepted philosophy, nor indeed an accepted code of ethics in public affairs within which to work. His 'comprehensive soul' had only its own vision to rely on, its divine instrument of the poetic imagination with which to probe the mystery of life and death; the challenge was of a tremendous urgency in his day, and he met it and triumphed; and one can say that what Shakespeare wrote has conditioned the whole subsequent development of English literature, has been its inspiration and its guiding star. To quote Theodore Spencer again:

> Shakespeare's vision of human life transcends anything given him by his time. The inherited concepts represent, of course, our particular

codification of what is permanently true about humanity, and when a civilization lacks such codification, that civilization is in danger. But Shakespeare's presentation of Hamlet, of Lear, of Cleopatra, of Imogen and Miranda goes deeper than any codification: it is the individual human life, the thing itself underlying codification that Shakespeare gives us, and which makes him, in Ben Jonson's familiar phrase, 'Not for an age but for all time'.*

I myself would go further than this: I would say that it is not merely the individual human life that he gives us, but the whole of human life in the rhythm of its birth, growth and decay, and in its relation to the unseen world that surrounds it, so that one may truly claim with Dryden that 'all the images of nature were still present to him', and believe that his work in its sum total is not merely a substitute for the codification whose collapse called it into being, but greater than any codifications that our way of thinking is likely to reach, containing them all within its heart. Not all of it is immediately comprehensible, for life itself is too complex to be immediately comprehensible, and a paradox and an obscure depth remain however deeply one explores into it; but Shakespeare, in the way of the poetic imagination, gives one precisely an image of what lies within the frontiers of rational understanding and what lies beyond them, so that one comes back again and again to Shakespeare after the testing of what is smaller and more confined—though perhaps more intense and wearing an appearance of greater novelty within its narrow bounds—to say to oneself: 'here is the larger and truer view, here is the vision which allows, by effortless instinctive rightness, for the factors which the others left out.'

It is of course impossible for me to illustrate this in detail from Shakespeare's work; it would be a subject for a whole book or a whole course of lectures, not for part of one, but the essential pattern for the purpose of my argument is this: in practically all his mature plays you find that the dramatic action arises out of a violent disturbance of the natural order, which works itself up to a climax where opposing forces are called forth and the original forces which caused the disturbance are finally destroyed—in the supreme tragedies, *Hamlet*, *Macbeth* and *Lear* at great cost, in the later romances with miraculous avoidance of the price that might

* *Shakespeare and the Nature of Man* (Cambridge University Press).

well have been paid. Everywhere is the warning against the fanatical, the obsessional, the attempt to impose too ruthlessly what goes against the human grain, the demonstration of the fatal course of the will or the intellect that refuses to allow for the heart, the headstrong temperament that cannot admit imperfection or mystery in life—the possibility of even the best human judgement being wrong by absolute standards. And all this is not a thesis that Shakespeare endeavours to prove to his reader or spectator, in fact it is the very opposite: it arises directly from the fact that, again as Dryden says, when Shakespeare describes anything, 'You more than see it, you feel it too'. And it is what William Wordsworth had in mind, when he observed that 'Aristotle, I have been told, has said, that Poetry is the most philosophic of all writings: it is so: its object is truth, not individual and local, but general and operative, not standing upon external testimony, but carried alive into the heart by passion; truth which is its own testimony, which gives competence and confidence to the tribunal to which it appeals, and receives them from the same tribunal. . . .'

This conception of poetry as something which discovers truth by its own methods, a truth 'not standing upon external testimony, but carried alive into the heart by passion' is Shakespeare's great gift to English literature—and I will say nothing here of his influence on German, French and Russian literature—so that if one can speak of a spirit of English poetry since that tremendous upheaval which destroyed the medieval world order, it is a Shakespearian spirit, something that would have been totally different and would never, I believe, have had that fertility and abundance which has astonished the world if Shakespeare had never lived. It is a thread we find winding its way through Milton and Dryden, through Wordsworth and Blake and Keats right up to our own time. And if I were asked to define the essence of this spirit, I would put it like this: in English poetry there is a continual reaffirmation of truths of supreme importance to our lives, to our civilization, which are outside the range of logical reason and have a reality and value far more permanent than any political or social or economic constructions can ever attain. These are what Jakob Burckhardt called 'the débris of the contingent'; English poetry does not deny the necessity for such constructions: it merely asserts that there are other, more fundamentally important things in the universe without the recognition of which the world of logical reason may become the darkest and most hopeless kind of dungeon.

No English poet after Shakespeare exemplifies more completely and effectively the working of this spirit than Wordsworth. One of his most famous sayings on the subject of poetry was that: 'All good poetry is the spontaneous overflow of powerful feelings: and though this be true, Poems to which any value can be attached were never produced on any variety of subjects but by a man who, being possessed of more than usual organic sensibility, had also thought long and deeply. . . .' It was this gift of 'organic sensibility', which one might perhaps describe as the power to apprehend the world sensuously and intuitively as well as intellectually, it was this gift that he came to cherish more and more as he grew older, something which he felt was in the liveliest danger from that 'excess of the selfish and calculating principle' which Shelley spoke of, and from the 'false secondary power' of reasoning divorced from feeling, the responsibility for which, in our civilization, Theodore Spencer puts squarely on Bacon's shoulders. Wordsworth did not learn this simply by quiet meditation among the lakes and mountains of Westmorland, but through direct experience of the central political and social event of his youth: the French Revolution. In his long autobiographical poem *The Prelude* he makes it quite clear how intoxicating the first stages of the upheaval in France were to his idealism:

> Bliss was it in that dawn to be alive,
> But to be young was very heaven! . . .
> Not favoured spots alone, but the whole earth
> The beauty wore of promise, that which sets
> (As at some moment might not be unfelt
> Among the bowers of Paradise itself)
> The budding rose above the rose full-blown. . . .

Wordsworth had been on a walking tour in France with a Cambridge friend in September 1790, and had seen the rejoicings of the people with his own eyes. He describes them brilliantly in *The Prelude*, and his subsequent sojourn in France at Orleans, where he went as soon as he had taken his degree at Cambridge. His enthusiasm was still at its height and he was determined to study the course of the Revolution at first-hand. He stayed, living between Orleans and Paris until 1793, when he returned to England just before war broke out, the war which was to last for nine years and cut him off altogether from the friends he had made in France and the woman to whom he had lost his heart. But he did not return to his own country the same enthusiast for the Revolution as he had set out. He had gone through terrible and alarming experiences when the September massacres broke out, of which we also catch a glimpse in *The Prelude*:

> It was a lamentable time for man. . . .
> Through months, through years, long after the last beat
> Of those atrocities, the hour of sleep
> To me came rarely charged with natural gifts,
> Such ghastly visions had I of despair
> And tyranny and implements of death,
> And innocent victims sinking under fear. . . .

He was a haunted man; but it was not until the war gave the Terror in France its opportunity and excuse and filled him with loathing for everything to do with the shape the Revolution had assumed, that the great change took place in his thought out of which his finest poetry was born. As we now know, he paid a secret visit to the girl who had meant so much to him, Annette Vallon, in 1802 before the new war with Napoleon broke out; and on his return the transformation was complete. England, he knew, was full of imperfection, corruption in high places and widespread apathy to great issues, but in spite of her faults he clung to her, he believed passionately in her cause in the war, because he felt that on his native soil there was still respect for moral tradition, still the possibility of following the intuitive guidance of the primal affections, which the iconoclastic fanatics of the Revolution had so fatally spurned in favour of the extremes of heartless logic. As one of the best recent critics of Wordsworth has written:

> The lesson to which Wordsworth had been deaf in 1793 had at length been brought home to him by the logic of events such as Burke had foreseen: he had come to perceive that a civil society is not a joint-stock company but a living organism, rooted in the past, and growing, if it truly grows, not by the application of abstract formulas about the imprescriptible rights of man, but by the laws of its own nature, which are embodied in its institutions and discoverable only from its history. . . .*

* *Wordsworth*, by Professor J. C. Smith (Oliver & Boyd).

Out of this cycle of experience grew the poet who was to develop his 'organic sensibility' in the greatest nature poetry of the nineteenth century, and his sense of the mystery and beauty of life, of all that could not be reached by the reasoning faculty alone, of all that escaped the purely material view of existence, in one of the most famous *Odes* in English poetry, *The Ode on the Intimations of Immortality from Recollections of Early Childhood*. It is such poetry which has most completely justified Matthew Arnold's claim that: 'More and more mankind will discover that we have to turn to poetry to interpret life for us, to console us, to sustain us. Without poetry, our science will appear incomplete; and most of what passes with us for religion and philosophy will be replaced by poetry. . . .'

Wordsworth's career has had a particular importance for many young poets in England during the last ten years, not merely because the situation in which he wrote his great series of national sonnets in 1802 so closely resembled the situation in which we found ourselves in 1940, but because they too had gone through political enthusiasms in the thirties not unlike his, had allowed their writing to be deflected to the service of political causes, and had emerged with a deep distrust of such entanglements for the creative artist. They came, like Wordsworth, to see that the poet's concern is elsewhere, and that the imagination can never be subservient to dogma or party, or the propaganda necessity of the moment.

The effect of poetry, of art on the lives of men will always be a subject of controversy, as it cannot ever be as directly apparent as the effect of an electric turbine on the lights of a town; but nevertheless I am convinced that as Newton's discoveries completely changed man's outlook on the physical world, and Einstein's discoveries are again changing that outlook today, so the work of the great poets has, in a far more profound and spiritual sense, completely conditioned the whole attitude to life and death, their value and their meaning, of the culture in whose veins their work like life-blood runs. The idea shapes history: and it is my belief that in the creation of the idea the work of the poet is the prime generative spark. Poetry works so secretly and so insensibly for the most part, that one cannot trace with anything approaching scientific satisfaction the tracks it makes, the flowers that burst into blossom in its path; but I will assert that as the great richness and vitality of English poetry for three hundred and fifty years is inconceivable without Shakespeare, so the course of English history, the English civilization we have inherited is inconceivable without that poetry; and Dryden and Wordsworth and Shelley and Matthew Arnold are the powerful witnesses I call to support my case. But not those great names alone—or others I might have quoted from other lands and other cultures—though it would indeed be strange if there were not a grain of truth among them when the conclusion they all come to is ultimately the same; not them alone, but all who have thought deeply about poetry and loved it until it is part of the air they breathe. Poets, one might say, are the lobes of balance we cannot do without in times of violent transformation and uncertainty, when old creeds are broken up and new false creeds eagerly grasped, are leading men into their hidden traps of despair; for to quote Wordsworth once more, the truth they offer us is 'not standing upon external testimony, but carried alive into the heart by passion; truth which is its own testimony, which gives competence and confidence to the tribunal to which it appeals, and receives them from the same tribunal'. If the great split between knowledge and morality is to be healed, if the masked and powerful anti-humanistic movements of our world are to be held in check, it will only be by the operation of the poetic imagination on the thought of men, by which the spiritual wells of our nature are kept fresh, and the 'visitations of divinity' are 'redeemed from decay'. That is the task the great poets of the past can accomplish for us—if we listen to them; but also the poets of our own times, if they preserve their freedom of spirit, for without creative freedom, under direction or the necessity of special pleading, the imagination as rapidly withers and dies as a tree whose roots can find no water.